MISSI

WWI TRUE STORY OF EVADING THE BRITISH NAVY TO SMUGGLE GUNS ON THE IRISH COAST.

WAR HISTORY JOURNALS

This book is based on true events. Some of the characters and events portrayed in this book are fictitious. Any similarity to real persons, living or dead, is coincidental and not intended by the author.

Where courage and judgement are equally required a clever coward is better than a stupid hero.

— Michael Collins

CONTENTS

INTRODUCTION

At the outbreak of World War I, Sir Roger Casement arranged a meeting in New York with Germany's top-ranking diplomat—Count Bernstorff. He proposed a plan that if Germany sold guns to the Irish Republican Army, the Irish would revolt against the English.

Sir Roger believed that "England's difficulty is Ireland's opportunity." This plan would divert troops, supplies, and attention from the western front. Bernstorff was intrigued and sent the message to the German high command in Berlin.

Over the next two years, Sir Roger negotiated with the German government for troops, weapons, cash, and supplies. The Germans refused to land troops on Irish shores, but agreed to supply the rebels with guns, ammunition, and supplies to support the uprising.

This is the true story of Captain Karl Spindler. A German sea captain ordered to smuggle 20,000 rifles, 1,000,000 rounds of ammunition, 10 machine guns, and explosives to the Southwest coast of Ireland. These weapons were vital to support the Easter Uprising of 1916.

An impossible mission suited for only the bravest and most fearless of men.

VOLUNTEERS STEP FORWARD

I just returned from an exhausting duty and planned to enjoy a cozy rest in my cabin. Away from this storm, maybe even a few hours of sleep. A knock at the door. A messenger brought an urgent note from my commander. I steadied myself on the rolling ship. The roar of a violent gale flared up on the sea. Bluish-gray clouds zipped across the sky. Rain battered window panes at every wild gust of air trying to rush in.

He wanted to see me at 5 p.m. I hoped the messenger brought the order to the wrong place, but the address confirmed it was for me. I knew this was not a good sign to receive such a formal invitation. The messenger probably read my mind when he told me that all the officers had similar orders. His comment relaxed me about the crime I may have committed. Maybe I had nothing to worry about? My mind raced in fear. *What was this about?*

The long walk in the flooding rain paid off.

Our ship was ordered to send a troop of volunteers. One officer, five petty officers and sixteen sailors, for an unknown military mission. The flotilla was instructed to send their best squad.

Every officer wanted to go. When the interviews finished, my chief gave me a sharp squint to tell he'd proposed me for the mission.

"What do you say?" he asked me. I couldn't refuse. My deepest desire was to be a part of an extraordinary operation. Now the opportunity knocked at my door. How could I say no? *I'm the luckiest man in the world.*

I wasn't given any details of the expedition. All crew members must be single men and have no dependents. My first sign we were chosen for an extraordinary task.

I gathered and addressed the men on my team at 5 a.m. I had no clue about the mission. I focused on the dangers of the job and told them not to rush to make up their minds.

When I was sure they had the idea of what they were chosen for, I gave the order: "Volunteers—three steps forward—march!"

I enjoyed the enthusiasm the men showed when they marched forward. They were ready to be a part of something exceptional. Something to be remembered by all others. The married men were left behind, even if they had dependents. A difficult choice. The crew of this mystery operation were not allowed to be more than twenty-two years old. After a hell of scrutinizing, I decided to take only strong, trustworthy, and brave men.

* * *

WHEN I RETURNED from four days of monotonous garrison duty, I learned I was the head of the *Libau*—the yet to be confirmed name of the mystery ship. I wasted no time gathering my men and getting into the inner harbor to report on-board. Commander Fortsmann, the leading head of the fleet, gave a curt and concise speech and bid us farewell.

We packed and made sure we left for the train before midday. Our mission still unknown. Was this a suicide mission? Were we going to be bait for a massive attack on the British? Everything was an "extreme hush." We weren't allowed to share information with our friends or companions. Any careless word caught by a spy could endanger the victory of our mission. We would stay silent even at the cost of our lives.

The next day, we reached Hamburg by train. Our new ship waited for us on the Elbe river. I was shocked at the sight of my new command. This wasn't the warship that would lead us to a swift victory over the British and seal my name in the records of history. This was a messy and mediocre British steamer. Not what I imagined. Not a patrol boat with the latest equipment. I glimpsed at the sad looks on my brave men's faces. We nodded to each other in disappointment.

I'd dreamed of commanding a ship-of-the-line. This wasn't it. This vessel was a large empty boat with elevated upper pieces standing high above the water. The port inspector *Hafenmeister* explained to me that the *Libau* was a new steamer from Britain and had the name *Castro* when she belonged to Wilson Line of Hull. We took her as a prize in the initial days of the war.

Everything was still in the same condition as when taken from the British. A jumble of odd bits and pieces, opened drawers, and papers littered the floor. The port repaired the boilers and engine and renovated berthing space for the sailors.

Besides this, the ship, the bridge, and the chart house looked neglected. How were we supposed to use this for our still-secret mission? How was I going to lead men on a British tramp steamer?

The next morning, we started the first stage of our expedition. No point of return for the volunteers now. We settled into the new rooms. Except for two men, we unloaded and set up into our quarters fast. The steward and cook were the exceptions—both excellent all around men—equally important as any on the ship.

For them, the *Libau* was a spacious, magnificent boat. They were used to working in over-crowded two-by-fours, with water up to their knees in rain and storms. Often utilizing both hands to hold the gear. Used to this painful athletic existence in the galleys, they found these wide quarters, big enough to accommodate as much space as needed. They shook and hunted, arranged, and re-arranged their belongings many times during the night.

Here I was, in my quarters. I spent the night pondering about the last two years. Such hard work, so many missions, sacrifice, and a blind obsession to following orders.

My dreams of glory and accomplishment were coming true. At 28, I was to become the commanding officer of an ocean-steamer. This goal was out of my grasp for so long, as if only a dream. But now, this dream was a reality. What would I do? Could I lead these men into the unknown? Would they respect me? Follow me? Die on my orders?

OUR MYSTERY SHIP

The next day we sailed toward Wilhelmshaven. When we arrived to complete the remaining preparations, the process was hurried. I chose two of my men to take care of the details. Besides my men and the dockyard guys, no one had access to the ship. Not even the highest-ranking officers.

On the shore, curious eyes scanned us as we moored beside the enormous *Mowe*. She'd returned after her first successful sea trial.

The equipment loaded on the ship—a great deal of it—was handled by men on the dock. All precautions to keep everything about the ship hidden were followed.

Despite every effort, we couldn't help but arouse curiosity in our neighboring ships. Our previous companions from the Outpost Flotilla were intrigued by our secrecy and mystery. I started a rumor we were setting off for Libau. To make it more authentic, I ordered our bows painted with the letters Libau. Our destination was unknown—even to me. One thing I was sure about was that wherever we were heading, it wasn't Libau.

With every passing hour, the secrecy grew. One of the hatchways that led to the hold was battened down, restricting entry to the entire crew. Just like in Hamburg, the ship was guarded at all times.

In one of the cabins, hidden under a sofa, was an entrance to a secret ship hold. Inside was a series of manholes and hidden ladders. The compartment extended from one side of the ship to another and had enough space to fit fifty men. Of its two ends, one made of iron bulkhead, the other made of wood. The wooden end covered it up well. It gave the impression of being made from iron and could have fooled anyone into thinking it was watertight and lacked any opening.

Whoever knew this secret could remove a plank or two and find a hidden escape route. Our ship had another compartment at a lower level than this one, used to house the excessive supply of coal, not to be made public during this mission.

Our mystery ship was full of surprises.

SIR ROGER CASEMENT

While the ship was being prepared, I was called to Berlin. I learned our destination was not Libau, and the head of the Irish Sinn Feiners was in Germany.

Sir Roger Casement was a passionate fanatic who despised England. He believed this world war blessed his country with a chance to liberate from English oppression. At that time, the Central Powers situation was promising, and Germany looked to be victorious. If the Irish decided to stand against England, they needed weapons to fight. The planned Easter uprising would offer the best chance for independence they ever had—or will ever have.

Sir Roger, from his writings, predicted this world war long ago, and the opportunity it would provide Ireland. Always a staunch supporter and a friend of Germany. To him, cooperation with Germany was the only hope of Ireland's deliverance. He promoted this idea through speech and writing, both pre and post-world war. Sir Roger claimed the support of a huge number of Irish, known as the "Sinn Fein Party."

The major financial support driving the movement was provided by Irish Republicans in the United States. Representatives of these Irish- Americans approached the German Ambassador in Washington months prior. They asked Count Bernstorff to forward their plea of German military support for the uprising in Ireland.

Germany refused to send ground forces but agreed to help with Count Bernstorff's proposal. She agreed to send a ship with arms and munitions to Ireland. This would serve as proof of Germany's willingness to help the oppressed Irish. And, if by any chance the Irish uprising was successful, it would shorten the duration of the war. England would be forced to withdraw her forces from the front, to curb the violent Irish uprising.

We planned our mission at the same time a naval demonstration on the east coast of England would be carried out. This was our opportunity to land arms and ammunition on the west coast of Ireland, while the British were distracted.

The ships' unloading on the docks and the successful Irish uprising depended on each other and posed a huge risk. Carrying out one without the other would render the whole operation futile.

After the return of the *Mowe*, successful in a recent breakthrough and attack on the auxiliary cruiser *Grief*. We believed blockade security would be tightened up.

The chance of running the blockade was not going to be easy. The Irish insisted on carrying out the uprising at Easter. According to the calendar, Easter translated to a full moon, the last thing I wanted when approaching the island. Sir Roger was in close contact with his countrymen across the water. He'd consulted them and assured us all the necessary precautions were taken.

We discussed the plan in every aspect with Sir Roger. I was selected for a task that demanded a high degree of courage and caution. I was happy. My chance to prove my heroism was here. I wouldn't let my men, my country, or the Irish down.

GOOD MORNING CAPTAIN

Sir Roger rejected the idea of going with us in the *Libau.* German high command decided to give him a submarine to use at his disposal. Sir Roger and his companions, an Irish sergeant, Bailey, and Lieutenant Monteith, would use the submarine to board the *Libau* at a meeting in Tralee Bay. I would move forward from there, per his directions.

To prevent the destination of *Libau* being exposed, I was instructed to exit Wilhelmshaven and move towards the Baltic. The trains carrying our arms and ammunitions were ordered to Lubeck on the following night by telegram. They arrived the same time as us. The railway authorities didn't know where they were headed. They kept trains waiting for days in different Central German stations.

* * *

We headed out at 2 p.m. The commanding officers of barriers and guardships had orders to not stop us from passing through. Once we passed the "Roter Sand" lighthouse, we brought up large boxes from a secret hatchway.

We passed out our Norwegian uniforms to the crew. Plain blue suits, sweaters, caps, linens, all original to their smallest detail. Even the blackish buttons were labeled from a Norwegian company.

We changed clothes and looked like Scandinavians within a few minutes. One of the stokers, a tall Bavarian, asked why the stokers didn't get fine large blades like the sailors. I explained to him that these were just for work and later on, all would have appropriate knives and guns.

After we took on our disguise we disposed of all military bearing and movement. To play our parts properly we had to familiarize ourselves with the tramp-transport ways. I assumed this would come simple to the men, but this was not the case. I couldn't resist a twinge of pride at how difficult it was for the men to dispose of their military polish.

After a little encouragement, they stopped all the heel-clicking and called me Cap'n, rather than *Herr Leutnant*. They spoke in a low German dialect that could pass for Norwegian. I let them grow their beards.

We flagged farewell to a gathering of ships on their way into the Elbe. In the night we went through the Kiel Canal. The next morning, we left the Bulk lightship, and we crossed through the Fehmarn Sound in bright spring weather. After a couple of hours, we were in Lübeck.

I'd chosen to accept my role of trader captain. Clad in the go-ashore pack suitable to my status. I arrived at the personal office of the trading port. I was welcomed with a courteous "Good morning, Captain"—a burning irritation surged through my body. I nodded, took a deep breath, pressed my eyes closed and chided myself for getting upset. I accepted the company's help and secret workers in the final fitting out of the *Libau*.

The packing of cargo posed a problem. I took into

consideration the amount of coal and water needed for our journey. Our draft would be overloaded, and if we had strong weather, we could capsize. We would have to take on less coal to make room for all the arms and ammunition we were transporting to Ireland.

The stevedores were busy with the coal, arrangements, and water. Afterward, they chipped away at loading freight. Piece by piece was carefully brought down into the hold. The cases were set apart with the standard dark and red shippers' imprints. The men must have suspected foul play. Why would a German payload liner have piece-merchandise with names like Genoa and Naples?

I informed a select few men that the *Libau* was going to Libau. Murmured from man to man under the strictest seal of mystery. This way I'd be certain it would get all around town. I let out once that I was going to take troops on board in Libau, and head to Finland after. That sounded believable. The next morning, one of the men I told in secret said several British and Russian strangers asked him about sending soldiers to Libau. I tried to force back a smile. I expected that the gossip would reach the ears of English spies. An ideal situation if the Russians had this misinformation as well.

In the *Libau's* front rooms were a wide range of certified Norwegian hardware. Stamped with the company name along with the latest Christiania papers and Norwegian books. We called the secret entrance to the hold through the sofa bunk, the "conjurer's box."

This hid our German hardware from snooping eyes. Our uniforms, arms, explosives, bombs, and German marine devices, were kept down in the secret hold. We had enough supplies to keep us well for six months—except for coal, we took on only forty-five days' worth.

We double checked what we still had out on deck. Any German object, even a pants button with the name of a German company on it, could double-cross us.

We had everything we wanted. Electric pocket-lights, instruments of every sort, bandages, paint, brushes, and sail material. Wood and concrete for different uses, curtains, bed-cloth, and ceramics. Everything a Norwegian boat would be given.

Our ships papers clearly represented us. We had a diverse supply of engine-room diaries, articles, and manifests. These would authenticate the ship, team, and payload, proving our validity past any doubt.

I was given a forged letter that urged our ship not to follow the usual liner track. It said that it was on this track German submarines had made such awful wreckage. This letter could convince the right type of English nitwit why I was following such an odd course.

After the freight of weapons had been moved aboard, we stowed the "cover load." Tin showers, enameled steel products in cases, wooden entryways, window outlines, and comparative valuable articles. These imprints, showed their goal as Genoa or Naples.

While we were being loaded, my first mate worked on giving the ship a conventional tramp look. The name *Libau* had been splattered out. Since the news about our planned arrival in Finland had got around, it could do no harm to hide our name.

I waited for news from Berlin, where major issues were still to be resolved. The mission may not happen. It would be decided in twenty-four hours. The next night, I got orders via telegraph to continue with the mission. My helplessness was finally over.

The next morning, we got ready for the ocean. We

waited for our final touches before we were to head out to sea. We waited for our dog. A dog is a must on a tramp liner. He came and now we were ready to make way.

We needed the help of a Norwegian language translator. I was given a pocket dictionary, but despite the lack of our linguistic knowledge, we were confident. We'd depend on our low German *Plattdeutsch* to pass ourselves off as Norwegians. The English were not linguistics masters. If we were boarded and the crew questioned by a Norwegian translator —we could get caught in our own web of lies.

THE NORWEGIAN AUD

The clock in a nearby church-tower rang six hits and strokes. The *Libau*, under the commercial flag, pulled out from the pier. A charming and quiet Sunday laid over the harbor. My men considered this a sign of something good to come.

We passed Travemünde in seconds when it got dark and dim. I was sad to leave this pleasant little town. I ordered the engine room full speed ahead. Our journey toward the unknown had begun.

Now was the time to brief the crew of our mission and journey's purpose. I avoided saying anything related to our course or destination. I left out most of the details I knew and dodged any specifics.

If any crew were taken as prisoners, they could say that they knew nothing. I gave everyone a Norwegian name and rating. Some names didn't translate well and were more than awkward. I told the crew that from now on, no German names. Everyone must get used to their new name and rating.

The men enthusiastically absorbed my information and

explanations. I chose the right men for this mission. We made all the items in our daily use—garments, flags, books, instruments—look old and well used. We altered the ship's documents, the different letters, and other documents on board to keep in line with our ruse. We used a smoky candle to make papers brown. We rubbed our hands with dust from under a mat. We made oil marks and greasy spots with cotton balls from the engine room. We folded and crumpled the papers to add to their final look.

We gave the books special treatment. We flung them on the floor, tore their corners, and removed parts of the paper leaves. We then repaired the torn, stained, books with gluing plaster. The facial hair craze inspired the men. In those who grew whiskers slower, we enhanced it with oil and coal dust.

On the hatches, I had chalk marks made and numerals painted, showing the previous inspectors had been passionate in their duties. Empty Norwegian meat tins and old Christiania papers were scattered in the berthing.

Our crew was aware of what was at stake. And the thousands of people that zealously waited for the appearance of the *Libau*. The crew was wild with anticipation. No one considered the danger that lay ahead. We were energized by one desire. Into and through the enemy's lair and afterward home again, covered with glory.

At midnight, the weather turned for the worse off the coast of Warnemünde. The rising ocean forced me to change plans. We'd no longer pass through the Sound as a Swede and transform into a Norwegian in the Kattegat.

We needed to repaint and to assume the Norwegian mask quickly. In this weather, it was impossible. We had to try. I ordered it attempted. Stages dangled over each side of the boat. Men worked by the light of their electric-powered pocket-lights. They painted and tinted the name *Aud-Norge* in letters a yard and a half long on the sides.

Our work was frequently disturbed by passing steamers and fishing boats. When they approached, we put out our electric powered lamps. The rising sea came over the stages and drenched us. Washing away our hard-fought painting attempts.

Unafraid and inspired by a few tots of spirits to keep out the cold. The men clung to their posts. By the morning, the work was completed. When the first ray of dawn appeared, the *Aud*, shaking in the Baltic swell, was ready for the final stroke of paint.

ALONG THE DANISH COAST

The flag of Norway flittered from the stern. After the sun rose, the *Aud* lifted anchor. We were now tramp sailors. We rolled in our walk, pulled on small pipes, and gushed with seaman-like expertise throughout the four quarters of the ship.

After crossing the Gjedser reef, we headed toward Falsterbö. We hung our lifeboats outward on the ship. More for our wellbeing and safety then because it was needed. At midnight, I anticipated being in enemy territory.

We busied ourselves with preparing the ship for a clash with the enemy. If we needed to explode the boat quickly, a significant number of explosives were hidden in a covering of concrete, three feet wide. The closer the enemy, the more we'd take with us with the impact of the blast. The blast wire was taken around corners and edges to the upper deck, hidden from peeping eyes. We hid our weapons, tools, and shells, on deck and underneath, in places that felt safe from exposure and getting damp.

Our chef had a splendid idea. On the assumption he'd be set free—even the angriest Englishman needs someone to cook—he concealed a huge amount of arms and crowbars under a mass of ashes in an incinerator. He assured us if it came to that, he'd set every one of us free.

In the entire ship, from the conduit to protective walls, was a hidden instrument of annihilation prepared to be used if the need arose. We hid Naval badges and flags with the same strategy.

Alcohol and related beverages were an easy matter. Enough provisions were within reach—great White Horse whiskey and Fine Old brandy—half unfilled bottles left enticingly open.

Our next procedure was "emergency station practice." The allocation of every man to his special post. We planned for a fire, enemy attack, and similar cases. It was vital to be prepared for any crises that could arise. We'd quickly hide every telescope, German sextant, diagrams and charts, documents and log-books, and other route essentials, and replace them with Norwegian ones.

If boarded, we'd pack all contraband into a huge sack that dangled on the bridge. One of the men would move with it to the galley where the waiting chef would transfer it along to the secret spot. All of this would take two minutes.

The decks and engine areas would be cleared for activity. Mathieson, familiar with a little Danish and Scandinavian in appearance, would take the helm on the bridge, to switch roles with the officer of the watch. A first's mate uniform was kept in the chart house, just in case.

One of the stokers had an easy sitting duty on the forehatch. Lazily smoking his pipe and irritating the dog until it started to bark. On the signal, crew members, except for the engineers and stokers, would move like snakes to their bunks and pretend to sleep.

Anyone watching the peaceful innocence depicted by

our grimy tramp would be deceived. We practiced mouth signs and a pre-arranged signal in case we had to sink the boat.

We moved along the Danish coast far from Falsterbö where we encountered our first obstacle. War boats of every type waited. Our current course would take us directly into their swarm.

NEW WIND AT THE KATTEGAT

A crewmember yelled, "Destroyer coming up toward the back." After a second, we heard the surge of a slayer's bow-wave, and the ringing of her message as she checked. *What the hell do they want?*

A voice underneath us asked, "Where are you from, Commander?"

With a nearby amplifier, a sub-lieutenant stood on the crossing of the moving ship, her pipes level with our upper deck. Close as she was to us, the officers of the guard stared at us through their glasses. The men on the deck gazed at us with surprise. Trying to not get exposed, I ordered my men to go below. I stood firm at the rail, shaking my head. I communicated to the sub-lieutenant that I didn't understand the German Language they spoke.

"Obviously," I could hear the little man complaining, "another stupid commander who cannot communicate in a civilized language!"

Now, as one more try, he was yelling at me through the megaphone in a scratching tone, "Where are you from? Reply?"

I shook my head again, it was everything I could do to not snicker when I recognized his accent. I'd spoken with him in the lanes of Kiel a few days ago.

He snarled and said something to a signalman. The sailor immediately ran toward the back, and returned with a lieutenant.

He yelled to me in familiar English, "Hallo, Cap'n, where are you coming from?"

"Danzig," I replied.

"Where are you destined for?"

"Christiania."

While he paused, I pretended to play with the dog, just to show I had no use for any further conversation.

In the break, I heard the sub-lieutenant, "Sense something strange here? This doesn't feel right."

I pulled on my gray-shaded scarf and took out my small pipe. I blew the debris into their eyes. Mathieson pushed his Norwegian-looking appearance into a closer view. He yelled over to the destroyer, "Okay, chief?"

They responded by flicking their hand in a signal I could understand meant, it was okay to depart.

We completed our first test. Five-hundred yards from the barrier, a Danish liner flying a pilot's flag came toward us. Our first real danger. No trader ships were permitted to go through the Flint-Rinne and the Sound without a pilot. I'd spoke about this with my officers and what we'd do about it. If a pilot boarded us, it would be challenging to maintain our deception of being Norwegians. If we refused his help, it may make others suspicious of us. My head pounded and my palms sweated as I had only seconds to make a decision.

Before he got too close, I made signs to show we didn't need a pilot. But the pilot insisted and continued on with signals and gestures that he was going to anyway.

I took the amplifier and yelled to him in English, "I don't need a pilot, I'm aware of the route." The pilot got even more upset and demanded a ladder to be put down for him.

Mathieson yelled to him in Danish, "We don't need you, we know the channel." Then I turned to port, he threw up his hands, his face twisted into a disgusted look and he steamed away. He headed for the Danish lightship at the passage to the Flint-Rinne.

The Danes were against the Germans. The lightship had a remote installation where they could report us to the English, "Questionable liner passed, continuing on a northerly course."

We waited in anticipation and dread for five hours after passing Helsingborg. No contact with an English cruiser. To make matters worse, we spotted a Danish yacht in the thin channel. She'd lain close toward the back of us at the piers of Lübeck when we were a German liner.

I could only hope that my luck was still holding out, and we'd get through this. Copenhagen and Malmö were far away now. We were greeted with a new wind at the Kattegat. A barquentine, under full sail, flew silently past us. She delivered no lights, and the spooky blueprint of her bellying canvas was outlined against the moonless sky. She vanished into profound obscurity.

Then, on the port side, the lines of a torpedo-vessel appeared. Searchlight beams darted through the air and vanished. Another glimmer upward, the cone bigger and bigger. He had us. On the decks of the *Aud*, it was light as day, our eyes blinded from the beams. A couple of moments and the cone vanished as fast as it came.

The Danish torpedo-vessel that watched the passage of the sound, held us for a second under a magnifying glass, looking at our markings—she passed us along as a harmless neutral ship.

HARD TO STARBOARD

Fifteen minutes passed since we crossed paths with the Danish torpedo-boat. Now, we were in enemy territory. We were alert. At any second, we might come face to face with an English cruiser, submarine, or destroyer.

Sightings of English submarines were reported between Lasö and the Sound, a few days back. We received reports about the presence of several English war-ships. Destroyers and the cruisers, sailing between Skagen and Göteborg, the Skager-Rack, and off the Norwegian coasts of Lindesnaes and Jäderen. At 2 p.m., we were five miles away from the east of the island of Anholt. I needed to make a critical decision.

The English had issued a notification that bound all the steamers to take a route within a ten miles radius of the Scandinavian coast. The purpose was to hurry the security clearance of each steamer with the English Warships. The small nations had no power to deny this rule, they had to obey. The only neutral who dared to go against the English was the Norwegian steamer, *Aud*.

I had two good reasons for this decision. Following the Swedish coast meant wasting a great deal of time. Second, I felt certain that the English would never expect a neutral would be daring enough to defy their orders. If we passed through the middle of Kattegat and Skager-Rack, it would give us a twenty-four hour head start. Maybe we could avoid the inspection altogether. It was a risk. We could get put under a deeper search and examination for defying their rules. We had to try. This struck me as the best choice of the two bad options available.

We set a course between the island of Lasö and Göteborg, to reach Skager-Rack a little higher up, in the north of Paternoster. This route had one drawback. If caught, no amount of lying could save us. All the permits we had weren't valid outside Christiana, our sailing port.

We depended on our luck. This risk was no greater than if we'd taken the assigned path and got vetted by an English-Norwegian interpreter. As soon as we lost sight of land and other ships, I ordered my crew to pick up the pace. My goal was to reach a path that verified the beginning of our journey from Christiana. If caught in the middle, it would be our end. If we made it out in time, we will have won.

The morning approached, the wind dropped, the sky still cloudy. A slight haze set in to the northwest, a harbinger of fog. If anyone wanted a fog at that moment it was me. We were all on the deck, looking for the slightest weather deviation. Those on watch below decided not to sleep. Every passing minute, the fog grew thicker. I stood near to the Swedish coast to determine our exact position by the shore bearings.

English war vessels patrolled the Norwegian coast in its entirety up to a point north of Bergen. At eight o'clock in the morning, the watch reported a ship sighting ahead. It was a small cruiser.

I called the situation an emergency. Everyone scrambled

to their designated posts. The cruiser was far off. It was near impossible to read its weather warped flag.

What would happen if she were English? Our papers had no information to support our presence in this area. A thought flashed in my mind, we had to do something. All this careful planning and hard work couldn't be lost now. The Irish depended on us. Germany needed us. My men depended on me.

I signaled my men to reduce the ship's speed and prepare the quarantine flag. I made them aware of my plan, and those not required at the deck moved to their quarters. Those who stayed on the bridge wrapped in thick cloaks up to their necks.

If the English ship approached, I'd hoist the quarantine flag and inform them we were en-route to Christiana from Danzig, suffering from diphtheria. I'd ask them to inform the port of our arrival and condition. There was a good chance they may not board us. To authenticate my strategy, I had a bottle of carbolic acid poured over the deck to mimic the sickbay odor.

The cruiser headed our way fast. In ten minutes, she'd be upon us. The situation was tense, everything relied on the success of our game. She took a sharp turn on a north-easterly course, her flags visible and revealed to our scared, anxious eyes—Swedish colors.

Our hearts lightened. In the blink of an eye, the sick felt well, and everything hidden was brought into the daylight. This dress rehearsal proved a success.

After a short while, behind the Swedish steamer, was the small island of Paternoster. We stayed a considerable distance from it to avoid English patrol inquiries. The fog cleared, and the coastline became visible toward the fore-end of the ship. I had an excellent chance to dock. Instead, I decided to continue sailing north before altering our route west.

By midday, we covered ample distance north and were now in a clear position to steer into the middle of the Skager Rack.

We took our bearing measurement by taking the mainland lighthouse into account. Along with a sounding to help determine our chart position. Afterward we headed west at full speed. If only the fog would last another six hours, we could confidently claim we hailed from Christiana. The angels above were again in our favor, the fog not only persisted but thickened.

The crew knew how much the situation depended on the speed of our vessel. They revved the engines as much as they could. At three o clock, we were alongside Skagen, and I set us on a southwesterly course.

To steer clear of a fog collision, we relied on our eyes and ears only. I relinquished use of the siren, a pin-drop silence on the deck. We heard the beat of the pistons, the gurgle of water at the bow, we drove our ship at twelve knots.

For two hours, we sailed at that pace until a high dark bulk appeared out of the blue, through the fog, a bark under full sails.

Hard a-starboard! The wheel swung at lightning speed. For a long moment, it felt like the maneuver failed. The *Aud* answered but the response was slow. Lucky for us, the other ship realized the situation, and steered hard over, missing us by fifty yards. The bark was hoisting a red rag of bunting, which must once have been a Norwegian flag, we cheered them as they sailed by.

By evening we were on such a good route it was easier for us to defend that we'd set off from Christiana. From now, we kept a Norwegian logbook. It could be checked as proof of our journey. We kept two logs, one for navigation, the other for the engine room. We started from our current position and traced back the distance to Christiana to determine the time we should have left. The time record as to where the pilot was dropped also had to be accounted for. All this information required to be filed under defined headings.

Our real course, positions, coal consumption, speeds, etc., would be different from the values mentioned in the Norwegian logbooks. Later on, it became complicated to maintain the thoroughness of these logs. These false entries were my introduction to the secrets of "double-entry bookkeeping."

MERIDIAN OF GREENWICH

The weather changed as it approached nine o clock. A light wind blew from the west and caused the fog to dissolve. Leaving behind a clear view and improved visibility. The moon rose but shined from behind the clouds. This made the shadow of our ship barely noticeable.

Midnight approached, we estimated that we should be alongside Lindesnaes. Here we expected the coast would be under close watch by the English. The traffic from all directions whether north, east, or west had to pass through this checkpoint in the southwestern corner of Norway. I ordered the mast headlights and side headlights lit. I had the lenses rubbed with soot, to dim the lights so they'd only be seen a ship's length away.

We could claim all the lamps on the ship worked and blame them for being dim, on the lamp trimmer. The remaining ship lights were carefully screened. We waited anxiously for hours before closing on Lindesnaes. Could we pass unnoticed?

A flash from the north. Above the horizon, four searchlights appeared, their beams made a crisscross pattern, illuminating our deck. One of the beams rested on us for a moment—we were caught. No, it passed over and lit the water behind us. This continued for five minutes but felt like an eternity. Every second the searchlight stopped. My stomach dropped to my knees. Then the beams rose high in the sky, concentrated eastward far from us. I ordered lights out and headed northwest for the open sea.

From then on, I kept in mind one important point while planning future courses. I'll keep a distance of at least a day's travel from Kirkwall Harbour. Where the English sent all suspicions ships. If we ever got caught and a prize crew deployed on our ship to take us to the harbor, twenty-four hours would give us enough time to gather resources, fight and reclaim our ship.

The next day passed, we encountered a couple of Dutch fishing boats and a Norwegian steamer. The steamer didn't like our looks. She left at once with the thickest cloud of smoke her furnaces could produce. She changed course after getting far from us. We found it better to pose as a hunter than prey.

After four days we saw the Grand English Fleet only a couple of times. I spent the night in the pilothouse, only leaving for a quick nap, when I was stirred from men yelling on the deck.

I heard shouts of, "Cloud of smoke on the port pillar."

Damn. What kind of ship was it? It could be a trader vessel, or a warship, we headed toward the Shetland cordon.

For fifteen minutes, nothing was visible except a huge cloud of smoke. Its thickness varied. It gave the impression of being produced from multiple furnaces. I sent my first mate to the top with a clear Zeiss glass. He returned with news of a high topmast with a spotting-top—the funnels not yet identified. A warship. The plot thickened.

I issued the order, "Everyone to emergency stations. Course northeast, engine-room lessen smoke." A northeast course was the best option, to avoid other warships on that path. We had no way to determine the cruiser's direction.

The "smokeless" stunt we tried was a success. The plan worked because these types of merchant ships were not equipped to handle smokeless fire. Only military men were trained for these circumstances.

The next moments passed by like a bomb timer ticking away our fate. The cruiser steamed toward us at full throttle, the topmast unrestrained, now seen from the deck and top.

"A second lower mast," reported the look-out. The position of the masts made it obvious the English ship was on a northeast course. I directed the ship four points to starboard, the goal that we were currently on an easterly course. Maybe we might get away.

The difference in mast heights meant we dealt with a newer and faster version of English cruisers. If she located us, any attempt at evasion was pointless. We hoped the English look-out would miss us. It was well known on watch duties that involve cruising for a long time in similar waters, hardly crossing paths with anything except the same ocean and sky—a sailor's watchfulness could get blunted.

Our luck prevailed again.

A call from overhead reported the cruiser was withdrawing. We watched her change course. The cruiser opted for the westerly course. This implied she'd not seen us. In a little while, no part of either mast would be visible, instead, only a pair of light wisps, or smoke on a foggy skyline. I couldn't believe our good fortune.

I found our position. We were seventy-five miles away in

the east of the Shetlands. A light bank of fog concealed the cruiser from us—nothing else visible to us in any direction.

Maybe she was the easternmost cruiser of the line. Only a couple of weeks prior, had nearly proved catastrophic to the returning *Möwe*. Maybe we were clear of the Shetland cordon. Did we escape the first barricade? Were we going to get out of the North Sea and into the Atlantic?

I had to choose our next course carefully. The most limited were between the Orkneys and the Faroe Isles. The more twisty course between the Faroes and Ireland would mean eight days steaming at a normal speed before arrival. This was also the main barricading power. Composed of enormous cruisers, patrolling over two-hundred miles of untamed water.

We could go around the north of Iceland. But this relied on the ice-conditions. I didn't have any data on the current conditions. So much relied on wind and climate that it would have been pointless to make arrangements over a day ahead. The course through Iceland and the Faroes offered the best opportunity. I chose to steam north and try to sneak past.

Toward the early afternoon the sky was cloudy, a fog not far off. We had to head in toward the coast, get our bearings by soundings or shore-course. We headed at max throttle for Bremanjerland on the Nordfjord.

Thirty minutes later, the haze bank in front of us lifted. A long, low dark dim hung on the water. It developed longer and higher until the outline of the coast appeared. The mist broke, the sun shone through and before ten minutes passed, a magnificent scene laid before us.

Dark blue water, smooth as a mirror, the breeze dropped, and snow-shrouded piles of Bremanjerland gloriously rose. In the mountainside hollows laid out zeniths of rock, snow flickering in the softening beams of the sun. To the east, the mountains were higher, a progression of icy masses. It looked as if we'd been shipped to the Alps. I hung on my course until I was close inshore. With the guide of my graphs and cruising headings, I found my current position.

The abrupt change in the climate played the devil with my plans. It would have been impossible to get through the Shetlands in a climate this clear. I chose to keep a good distance away—a few hundred miles north-east of the Faroes—where the Polar Circle converges on the meridian of Greenwich.

CALM LIES THE SEA

The next day at 4 o'clock we arrived. The air was clear, the sea quiet, no signals of any change. Up till now, we hadn't seen any ice. But as we neared the Arctic Ocean edge, the path north around Iceland wasn't possible. The ice hadn't yet broken into pieces.

The full moon approached. In these high latitudes no night existed. I ceased the engines and waited to see in the coming days. This type of weather couldn't last long. My rendezvous in Ireland was still days away, I had time. This was the perfect place to hide. No ship in their right mind would venture this far north.

The only danger up here would come from our submarines. They were not told of our mission and had no details of our journey.

We took this time to make required repairs and maintenance on the ship. This was serious business, we had no idea of what major tasks we'd need to put the ship through in the coming days.

The deck-hands repainted flags and the calligraphy on

our sides. The weather and water had turned our ship's name and markings into a mystery of dots and sprinkles. The pressing issue was how to handle the next twenty four hours. I called a meeting with my officers in our small canteen area.

We must pass through the English line in front of us or travel north around Iceland. The route around Iceland was the most dangerous. A natural barricade, we ran the risk of running into ice and sinking. Our ship was not built our equipped to handle that passage. Our alternative was to try and sneak by at least ten English cruisers.

The path toward the Faroes from Iceland was close to two-hundred nautical miles. We could count on an average speed of fifteen knots. Without thick foggy weather, it was foolish to assume we could slip through. The gaps between the guarding cruisers would be tight and well-guarded.

I spent the night pondering and calculating potential courses. Every accessible outline and sail heading were claimed. I leaned over diagrams and charts with pencils and dividers. I considered arguments and points of contentions. We must get through. It was the best, *worst* option. We'd try the next day—hopefully with the weather in our favor.

* * *

A WHISTLE down the voice-pipe near my bunk.

"What is it?" I rubbed my eyes and sat up on my bunk.

"Waterspout to starboard. Captain, come up here quickly," yelled a man from the bridge. I hustled to the deck. A big dark section of water, over five yards in diameter, with less width in the center, raised into the clouds.

It moved fast through the tranquil water, hovering over

the surface. Its power thrusted from the whirlpool at its base, shooting up an angry foam.

We avoided it and turned hard to port. If we had gotten close to its path, we'd have been torn to shreds.

KEEP A SHARP WATCH

The temperature plummeted. Messy dark tempest mists rose from the west. Vivid cat's-paws showed up on the water, from the north or west, and then from a south-west. A change in weather was coming. The first mate looked through the skyline with his spectacles and mumbled to himself.

I walked to the helm and strained to see off in the distance. "I bet it's a north-wester. Do you smell it? Rainy and foggy weather is coming."

He crinkled his lips into a frown. "I don't think so. It looks like a—"

A wave of irritation swept over me. "I can smell the haze coming. Sit back and watch."

* * *

AT 8 O'CLOCK, a dull shadow appeared on the water toward the south. My hand shook as I reached for my spectacles. *Wind.* A south wind—exactly what we'd hoped for. In a couple of moments it will reach us. The water rippled from the fresh, cool air. The skyline faltered.

The division among ocean and sky appeared heaved and swelled—promising a coming mist. At 10 o'clock the breeze bounced toward the south-west and renewed. Light wisps of fume floated down our port bow. After thirty minutes the skyline shrunk to the point it was tricky to see.

"Orders, Captain?" the watch asked. He gave me a sharp look.

"Continue," I said. "Half pace. Route south-west."

The motor room and stokehold energized. The screw spun, foam agitated in our wake, the *Aud* got underway. The chart house was a free-for-all of computing and estimating. We chose to continue at a reduced speed on a northern course. If when we reached that point, the weather was still foggy and misty, we'd make our leap and sneak by the English.

By early afternoon we evaluated the quality of the breeze as 3. Occasional light showers of a fine downpour. Still a day's steam from the English line. This timing was perfect, the moon darkened by mists. The temperature gauge fell. The current was still too high to mean a quick storm. If the temperature kept falling at this rate, a tempest could lay ahead. I chose a southern course—through the barricade.

We multiplied the watches. Even the chef needed to stand watch. Our watch motto was: "Keep your eyes prepared." In front of us waited a fleet of English cruisers.

* * *

The next day was April 16. At 4 a.m. I entered into the logbook "Cloudy, foggy, periodic overwhelming showers, twist, south-west 4, refreshing, relating ocean."

We figured out the route and the path length. It was one-hundred-fifty nautical miles to the line were the enemy waited. If we pointed straight for the center of this line, we should arrive by 8 p.m. on Sunday.

We counted on the enemy being somewhat distracted. We hoped the English sailors dug into their alcohol rations and were not focusing on their tedious duty. With the cloudy and ominous weather, it would be pitch dark by 8 o'clock. Before dawn, we could cover sixty miles and be out of sight.

The farther west we steamed, the ocean grew in cold air and power. The rain came over the bows and we huddled into our oilskin clothes. The afternoon was a pleasant shock. The downpour turned into a haze. At about 4 p.m. We couldn't see eight-hundred yards in front of us. Our situation improved by the minute. How did we get so lucky?

We moved south-west at our maximum speed. Anybody who watched us would have thought we entered out of the Polar Sea. If an English ship came out of the haze near us, it would be difficult to make them believe—we were a tramp steamer carrying coal.

Until 6 o'clock we could only see three or four boat lengths ahead. Our crew was alert. None of the men rested. They stayed vigilant. The haze over the water lingered, dark and overwhelming. The strange tranquility rattled our energized nerves. We never took our binoculars away from our eyes, even for a moment. Every second we listened and looked for something strange. Large white caps crashed the *Aud's* bow, splashing over scaffold and vessel. Each spray of water on the bow enhanced my stress as we approached the English line.

"What's the Time?" I asked.

"Ten past seven, Captain," the watch answered.

"Keep a sharp watch. We're near the line."

* * *

THE CLOCK's hands struck 7:15 p.m. The ship came alive with activity. Starboard, a dull, dark dim matter appeared out of the haze.

"Hard a-port," I yelled. "Speed up to maximum. Emergency stations."

The wheel moved fast to port with such a sharp movement, the wiring in the motor room transmitter creaked as if it was damaged. Like a shocked sea-bird runs away, the *Aud* darted in a quick bend to port.

Damn. An English cruiser. Her shape appeared—two masts, high upper works, a thick channel.

"Half pace. Route, south-by-west," I ordered.

We couldn't run. We were exposed to the English ship. I estimated her at a distance of two hundred yards. If she continued on her current course, she'd be side by side us in minutes. The fun begins.

At the initial alert, the watch beneath—observing on the deck—moved toward their bunks. We stood on the scaffold. My heart thumped in my chest. The crew fell into their tramp sailor routine: calm and collected, hands in pockets, spitting and smoking. We made sure to show no obvious anxiety to the cruiser.

We continued to stare with our spectacles, tooting every few minutes, like the freighter we were. To the outsider, we were a harmless tramp steamer. We steamed next to the

English cruiser for what seemed like an eternity without communication.

I was desperate to know what the English ship was doing. They studied us with their binoculars. I sent my first officer to the chart house. Through the chart house window he could better describe the English Cruiser to me.

"Many huge weapons forward—same aft," his voice rattled.

On the cruiser, men stood at the deck, staring hard at us.

We waited for a command from the English ship. Were they going to order us to stop? Fire blanks at us? Nothing. Will they follow us into the Faroes? Those rocky islands lay ahead. One more day's steam from here.

Time slipped by. We waited, making ourselves ready for whatever may happen. At 7:30 p.m. I ordered "7 rings" hit on the boat's bell. The sailor who observed us at the cruiser's rail slunk away. Was the English cruiser losing interest in us? It was cold out and wet all around the deck, and at eight the watch will be changed. Did he climb below for a tot of steaming grog?

The sun fell into the horizon and dusk would be soon upon us. I gave instructions to light the masthead and side-lights. Our fake paperwork laid organized on the flag-locker. No action or movement on the English cruiser. Even the bridge was left to only the watch officers.

Did the English ship think we were a harmless tramp? How could they not have any questions about why we approached from the north?

Eight bells rang. Time for the watch change. New guards scurried to their positions on the deck. She was so near to our ship that we saw everything happening on board even while the sun set. If only we had a torpedo or a submarine to help us. One torpedo to the English cruiser would destroy her.

Maybe it was too cold for the sailors. They might shadow us as we traveled southward. If they tried to board, we could manage them.

I couldn't figure out why or what they intended to do. I could gesture to them with our Morse light and request our position. I needed to get information from them. Something, anything about their intentions.

The English ship picked up her pace and moved three-hundred yards ahead of us. She put her rudder over hard and swung over our bow on an SSE course. The English cruiser had no intention of getting closer to us. She disappeared into the thick dull haze. I strained to see her through the haze. Nothing.

"The English are gone." The men shouted and clapped.

We needed to get out of there as fast as possible. I ordered, "maximum speed ahead." We smothered the lights and as fast as we could, we headed northwest.

We needed to get away from the cruiser line as fast as possible. We spent the next three hours on our course until I dared to head west once more.

We were in the North Atlantic—getting closer to Ireland.

* * *

AT MIDNIGHT, the wind blew so intense we needed to tie down everything not bolted into the deck. I had lifelines drawn-out to clutch. The breeze swerved toward the west, and then north-west. The haze had gone. A downpour drenched us. The temperature plummeted. These were signs of an approaching north-wester.

The little *Aud* whipped through the puzzled ocean, shaking off the water washing over her bows. Her unsharpened bows and upper-works protected us from the cold wind. Our speed reduced from ten knots to five, and later to four, until we barely moved at all.

I put her on a southerly course, trying to stay clear of the English barricade westbound of the Hebrides. Even in the densest haze, one was never safe from the English. No guarantees that our next encounter with the English would go in our favor.

The Breeze came from the north-west. By the middle of the day, the breeze was battering us and testing the strength of our ship. I was confident our ship was strong and seaworthy enough to brave a violent storm. The cargo worried me. The ammunition was not stored in the safest way. With the ocean crashing over us, we couldn't re-stow it. The holds would fill with water the moment they opened.

The ocean swirled. Wind gusts followed each other. A storm brewed.

The last two days shuffled us to a place far outside of our chosen route. Were we still by Iceland or slingshot toward the Irish coast? I had to get our bearings. We needed to make our landfall at the correct, agreed upon location. I couldn't risk feeling my way down the Irish shore. After some intense navigational work, I discovered we were a day away from the Rockalls.

Hidden from the Atlantic, over two-hundred nautical miles west of the Scottish seaboard, was a far-extending reef. The Rockalls were a sandbank with thousands of little rocks shooting up through it. The seashore has a distance of three nautical miles and runs east and west. At its western end, a single stone juts from the water. This solitary stone is the size of a conventional two-story house.

This stone is the main clear part of the reef, and the various edges are safe.

Where the bank closes, the floor of the Atlantic drops out of nowhere two thousand yards. Even on the large English maps, the Rockalls are set apart with a point the size of a pin's head. Many boats have been destroyed on these stones and die with all hands. It's a sea cemetery. The soundings which the graphs give on the banks are few. A small number of sailors have braved the Rockalls to chart it correctly. Common sense was to stay clear of it. I welcomed this challenge. I steeled my nerves and set my route for the western limit of the coastline.

The storm wailed. Wind gusts peppered us with volleys of hailstones. The ocean seethed against us. The haze and mist transformed into a downpour adding to the night's darkness. It was pitch black out and impossible to see anything. Then, out of nowhere, through a crack in the mists, the moon shone.

Off the starboard bow, a dull shadow appeared. A long, lean structure with a few promenade decks, two high slender channels, and two poles. Was it a Traveler liner or an English cruiser? It was too dull to tell.

I decreased speed right away. We had to disregard the thrashing ocean that swamped our ship. A sudden hail-shower cloaked us. The liner had no lights and steamed at a moderate speed. My gut told me she was a lookout cruiser—but I needed to be sure.

We waited on edge for another fifteen minutes. Out of nowhere, the liner appeared to wake up. She sped up and steamed away. We were now separated by more than a mile. Our luck held out again. She must not have seen us. So much for the famous watchfulness of the English armada. We slipped through their net again.

A WITCH'S CAULDRON

The storm became more intense. The roaring sea threw every one of us around the ship and tried to sweep away every movable thing on board. The vessel sides were getting battered. I ordered the crew to spread oil on water to reduce the damage. I changed course toward the South. We were able to decrease the roll and break the combers before they became too harsh.

At dawn, we saw the Rockalls ahead. One rock above the water—the only thing visible—the tides surfed when the columns of water shot up while seagulls circled it. The weather was getting wilder. Rain and hail over the mountainous ocean made it hard to see anything at all.

Since 8 a.m. I led us toward the other side of the bank. We saw the rock two miles away towards the east.

At 11 a.m. the raging sea had developed more deep tides on a shallow bank. Were we there? No one dared to claim it, but everyone searched for the bank through binoculars. We could not see anything, no surf, no rock, no birds.

It was noon. We had to be there soon. "Not reached yet," came the reply from the sounding machine used under the supervision of first-officer. Several reports came in of men thrown against the rail when caught by the sea. I ordered my men through the megaphone to stop and pour more oil on the decks.

Someone shouted the bottom was sixty-three units away.

"Slow down and focus more." I hollered through the megaphone.

We all knew what was at stake. Fifty, fifty-six, sixty-two, seventy, twenty, eight. *Damn*. A special chart under the glass cover on the bridge showed every fathom depth. It warned that these measurements were inaccurate.

Should we change course? But to which side? I didn't have time to think. I could risk the lives of my men and jeopardize the mission by driving into the stretch of reefs ahead. All the routes were alike until we saw the rock at a visibility range of 800-1000 yards. A temporary fear and hesitancy washed over me. I gathered my courage to hold on.

A man on watch at the lower bridge shouted, "Breakers to starboard."

"Hard a-port. Hard over." I shouted to the helmsman.

The ship slowly reacted to her tiller. The time extended from seconds to minutes. We tried to find the position of the breakers by covering our faces with our hands from the water and wind. We only saw a nonstop foam flurry. The surrounding tides were as high as a house. They spit thunder and spread water through the air like projectiles. I couldn't tell if the tide was splitting between the reef or the breaking ocean.

The *Aud* held on through this brewing hell. We moved on an eastern route toward where the sea took us to the port-quarter. The stern of the boat was getting punished by the waves. We increased the ships speed to no effect.

We couldn't tell if the breakers hit our starboard. We were still among the sunken sandbanks and reefs. We imagined them as dark eddies and patches in the water because of the dive in the breaking sea. The heavy rainfall and spindrift during the storm blurred our view. It was like we were watching the events unfold from behind a veil.

The sea leapt on the *Aud* over the starboard side. I thought she'd never be able to recover. After every roll our port side was underwater—but we recovered. Two birds appeared two hundred yards off the starboard lower on the sea. Rocks must be close.

"Port the helm," I said with too much anxiety in my voice.

"The compass," the quartermaster shouted. He held onto the shaft with a frantic hold, trying to keep the wheel hard over. Had our luck run out? The compass had gone mad. It spun like a teetotum, whirling faster and faster. Only the direction of the seas told us our heading was coming to port. We had to steer by the running seas, the compass was hopeless. One moment it pointed north, the next south-south-west.

The shouts of the aft leadsmen were gibberish. He tried to show us the soundings by making signs with his fingers. It was useless because of the depth distance.

Birds showed up on our starboard side. Then a whole flock whirled in the air. I had no doubt. Toward the south were sharp rocks waiting to sink us. We were on the edge of destruction.

"Hard a-port. Quick, man, quick," I screamed with all the strength in my lungs. I pointed toward port in vain—no one understood anything. It was the worst phase of the hurricane. The wind howled and whistled like a banshee screaming in combat—no one could hear anything.

The first officer had already put the helm hard over before waiting for orders. He saved us. This was the only chance we had to clear the reefs. We rushed into a foaming, fierce swirl waiting to suck us to the bottom. The engines were at full speed. We had only one route open to deliver us from this savage whirlpool. We squeaked by the swirling destruction by a matter of yards.

I looked back at the witches' cauldron we just passed. *We made it.* Our luck held out again. My body shuttered. I looked at my men, we were alive. I had no idea of the type of danger we were in. I couldn't tell if it was rain, sweat, or tears that ran down my cheek into the corner of my mouth. I nodded to the first officer and the quartermaster. We were alive. We had survived the deadliest and most fatal danger we had come up against since we started this mission.

As if the previous gamble wasn't enough, wild hail gusts began to pelt us. They were like mountains of water that came in a locust of rain. Like monsters showing open jaws to their prey, these water mountains raged against our ship, hurling over the deck and threatening to engulf us. Every wood of the *Aud* trembled and shuddered. At every new assault it seemed our ship would break apart.

Leadsmen with their lifelines stood on the aft deck in their drenched oilskins. They refused to leave their positions, despite being tossed around and ordered by my hand signals to move forward.

"Thirty-three fathoms," The first officer shouted.

Then, "Twenty-eight fathoms—twenty-three—eighteen—fifteen—twelve—eight." A sudden fierce shock rattled the ship. It shook the masts, funnel, derricks, deck-houses, ventilators, and the whole ship for several seconds. Everything trembled.

My first thought was that we ran aground. The chief

engineer rushed up through the ladder, panting. He reported no water in the engine room. He believed we'd run aground. I put the helm over to port and then to starboard —all in vain. The ship didn't move an inch.

The reason dawned on me.

A large amount of sea water came aboard and jammed the scuttles and stopped the scuppers. This water weighed down the ship and we couldn't move with all the extra weight. We missed this because our focus was on the possible reef off of starboard. Did any of my men get swept overboard?

Several minutes passed before the *Aud* answered her steerage. When she did, our spirits soared. If we could hang onto this north-easterly route for a while longer, we'd be free from the reefs. Luckily, we had a few hours of sunlight before us.

For two hours the *Aud* fought against the thunderstorm. It seemed as if we'd be overpowered. Then the gust receded. In less than an hour the ocean had calmed. The worst of it was behind us.

We'd made it out of the danger zone. We started to steam at a moderate speed on an easterly course. The compass worked again. I couldn't figure out if was the vibrations from the violent ocean or the iron in the reef that disabled our compass.

COMING OUT OF THE STORM

Night dawned and the breeze changed into a NW direction. We passed two other English cruisers—neither of them noticed us. How could this happen? Was it luck? Did the English know our plans? Were they waiting to capture us on the Irish coast?

My orders were to meet at the rendezvous point in twenty-four hours. After consulting my quartermaster and reviewing the charts again, we would arrive at Tralee Bay one day too early. I slowed our pace and took a southeastern course. I traced the route with my finger on the chart following the Irish coast.

A loud knock at the frame of the bridge door got my attention. I nodded at the signalman to speak.

"Captain, another English cruiser."

"Where?" I asked.

"Just over three miles off our starboard bow." The signalman pointed at a dull gray outline on the horizon. "We watched her come out of the storm."

I grabbed the binoculars and studied the shape. She was a long dark steamer coming at us fast. I ordered the men to emergency stations. And to double check the "bag of tricks" and "Conjurer's box" were stowed away and watertight. I stepped out onto the deck for a better look at the English ship moving at us like a bullet. The dog barked and jumped in circles on the forecastle.

The English cruiser stopped her engines five-hundred yards from us. I kept the *Aud* on her current course and reduced our speed to five knots. The more distance we kept this cruiser from us the better off we were. English blue-jackets crowded the rail. Her 3-inch guns were leveled at us. She slowly closed the gap and examined our starboard side. Then she passed through our stern wake and laid to our port side.

I crept us ahead, trying to increase our distance. The English sailors stared at us like we were some foreign animal creature. The English ship increased her speed and almost touched our port side. Then she shifted off on a fast eastward course.

"I don't understand this." The first mate said. "Captain, should we speed up for Tralee?"

Why didn't they question us? "Yes, maximum speed. Set a course for Tralee bay."

Were they incompetent? Why did they sniff us out and leave? Something doesn't feel right here. It had to be a trap.

* * *

THE TEMPERATURE GAUGE ROSE. The sun rays spread over the water and a soothing warm air thawed our souls and heightened our spirits. I organized a meeting with my officers to plan our strategy for the upcoming days. We decided to change our appearance once again. We'd move the chart house to the engine room. This would camouflage us in case they tried to identify us. We'd also shade our pipes and ventilators in darker colors with a yellow theme. We'd continue this journey under the flag of Spain. When we arrived on the Irish coast to meet Sir Roger, we would be ready to transfer our cargo.

We had no way to contact Tralee or the submarine carrying the Irish rebels. Would the western coast of Ireland have the same problems and restrictions as Dublin? On the east coast of the Irish shore and in the main ports, military law was in effect. If every coast of Ireland was under a tight, strict military law—our plans were in jeopardy. The smart move was to hold back and see how things developed. We would be in the right place at the precise time and deal with the events as they unfolded.

We gathered our weapons and cleaned them for use. We had four machine guns ready to fight with if boarded by an English prize crew. We created dummy guns to scare and intimidate any threatening ships. We made replicas of six 10.5 cm guns. While we had no ammunition or even real guns, we'd fire the machine guns and make a back splash to scare off any enemies.

I gathered the crew and filled them in on all the details. It was time they all knew what they were in for and the goal of our mission. The men were excited and ready. They shouted in enthusiasm and shook each other's shoulders.

The lookout shouted, "Submarine, four points off the port bow."

I strained to see a dark shape moving a few inches over the water. Were they German? English? I had to be sure. "Increase speed," I ordered. "Crisscross route. Watch out for torpedo wake."

We moved closer to verify. Fifteen hundred yards, twelve hundred yards, eight hundred yards—closer and closer. We verified the periscope as an unfilled preserved meat can in the water's wake.

* * *

APRIL 20 WAS a fresh and glorious Thursday morning. We were getting closer to the western coast of the Irish seaboard. The wind stopped and the warm air was still. The northwesterly waves were the only movement on the water. We finished the false covering and fake marking repaint through the night.

We dug out the arms and ammunition and prepared them for the transfer at Tralee bay. We opened the hatches and tossed any unneeded freight off the ship. In less than a half hour, the deck looked like a department store. Door and window frames, zinc buckets, tin baths were all dumped over the side in a steady stream. Our route was littered with debris that lined the horizon. I kept a couple of props on board for the next day, as a precaution.

At noon, our position read 52° N. 11° W—only forty-five miles from Tralee. We would be there in under four hours. The next two hours we busied with landing preparations. We uncovered the entrances, prepared the steam winches and unloading blocks for a quick landing.

If everything went to plan, we could be in and out in less than eight hours. I expected a problem when we reached the bay. The military and harbor authorities would inspect us and our papers. They'd ask questions about our departure country and could be relentless if not satisfied by our answers.

Tralee was three miles from the harbor rendezvous. The harbor was called the Fenit, connected to Tralee via a railway. If the alarm was rung, we could expect English soldiers in less than thirty minutes. We had our four machine guns to use against them. We could open some of the weapons cargo meant for the Irish and use that in the fight if necessary. I laid out explosives on the bow and had them wired and ready-to-use if needed. I set the German naval flag at the ready, in case we needed to show our true colors.

I ordered my men to clean up before putting on the Norwegian uniforms. Each man had a dirk and a pistol shoved into his belt. After one o'clock the coastline appeared. Bluish cloud banks and a long low-lying horizon signified the Irish coast.

I gave my men the final briefing. The engineers would pump out water tanks to reduce weight in order to get into the shallow Fenit channel. I distributed first aid boxes and bandages throughout the ship.

I made the men understand that if caught, I couldn't save them. They would be killed. The men laughed and joked, "the English would have to catch us first." I picked the right men for this job. I ordered every man to his place.

RENDEZVOUS AT TRALEE BAY

Brilliant sunshine welcomed us as we approached. Colossal, overhanging cliffs jutted out over two hundred yards from the water. Green grass patches and low shrubs littered the jagged, indented ridges of high ranged hills. The islands and offshore rocks came into view. Was there a more dangerous or inhospitable coast than here?

I instructed our lookout to search for any lighthouses, farm houses, any sign of life on the coast. Nothing, only bare rocks. I checked my course against the chart—we were close. This must be the bay of Tralee. We hunted for the entrance. In less than fifteen minutes, we found a small rock known as "Three Sisters" to the southern side. The coast bent sharply to the north east, then into a broad curve to the north west. The back of the bay was concealed, but the coastal line stretched from the sea. I changed course and looped in toward "Three Sisters."

A small triangular patch in the distance glinted off our port bow. It looked like an outline of a distant sail. Was it the Irish waiting for us? I wouldn't allow myself to get excited. Our navigator informed me that we were heading for the island of Loop Head. I changed our path to starboard. I saw bare sharp rocks poking out of the water. I scanned the horizon with my binoculars. The current yanked us inshore. We adjusted in small increments and figured out that "Three Sisters" was now two miles off the starboard beam.

Two hundred feet above the water over a broad cliff was a high signal mast with wireless aerials. A half dozen black muzzles peered off the aft of their ship. *Damn.* Maybe they wouldn't notice us? I sent all the men below who weren't needed on deck. The ship continued to approach. No signal or shot. Small islands came into view. Wretched little houses and shaggy fisherman appeared on the sides of the bay. The outlying homes and residents of Fenit stared at us from the shore. We headed into the island of Inishtooskert.

On the starboard side, a light colored tower that looked like an old castle stood on the skyline of the mountains. We steamed closer to our goal. Nothing moved, it was too quiet. An eerie feeling swept through me. Still no movement anywhere. The other ship was out of sight. I reconfirmed again that I was in the right place. We waited. Where were the Irish?

I reread my secret orders again:

"If you arrive and wait for over two hours with no sign of life nor communication. You may wait, proceed further or turn back. The decision is in your hands."

What would I do? Surrender and go back? *No chance.* I wouldn't give up under any circumstances as long as there was a sliver of hope. With no communication I was trapped. This was senseless. Something was wrong. My crew crowded around me on deck. I told the men of our situation. Not a single man wanted to turn back until we achieved our mission.

Two hours, six hours, the night passed. Did the Irish fail

to decipher the original message. Was the Irish rebellion already put down? Were the Sinn Feiners all caught and in an English jail? Or executed? My mind raced with possibilities. Was there a blockade and the Irish waited somewhere else to meet us? Where the hell was Sir Roger Casement?

I couldn't wait here any longer. I'd explore the bay and find answers. At a slow speed I passed between Fenit and Kerry Head. I reached the northern side of Inishtooskert. I checked for signs of life—no people anywhere. We came upon the Fenit lighthouse. It was a depressing sight. No sentry, the lighthouse sat on top of high naked hills surrounding the bay.

I continued on. In the back of my mind the thought that this could be a trap rattled in my brain. We steamed around the island, looking for signs of life. The day turned into another night. The moon lit our way as we returned to our rendezvous point for another pass. Would the Irish be waiting for us when we returned? We passed another night without contact from the Irish. I hated the idea of turning back. Why retreat? How long could we stay here before being discovered by the military?

One of my men shouted, "Steamer off the starboard bow."

I hurried out to the deck and leaned on the rail. Was it carrying the pilot to get us through Kerry's Head? I waited for a better look before ordering which signal to hoist. The steamer had a British flag instead of an Irish one. I nodded to my first mate and hustled off to my cabin. We had trained for this scenario and the officer of the watch knew what to do.

I peered out from behind a curtain in my cabin. Movement on the deck. I checked my watch, 5 a.m. The English ship was not in a hurry. She got closer and then circled us several times. Their crew analyzed us with binoculars. A uniformed British officer stood on the deck of his ship with a megaphone in hand. His men stood next to him, armed with pistols and rifles.

WHISKEY FOR THE ENGLISH CAPTAIN

"Where are you from?" The English captain yelled over.

Silence.

"Hallo, I say, where are you from?"

The first mate remained quiet.

"*Goddamn it*—Where are you from?" The English captain shouted.

The first mate answered, "Good morning."

"Damn it to hell man, save your formalities. What is your origin?"

"Identify yourself, sir." The first mate answered.

"I am the commander of this ship. Are you the captain?"

"No sir, I am the first mate."

"Where is your captain?"

"He is asleep."

"Well, wake him at once."

The first mate strolled to the gunwale of the ship and leaned on the lifeline, "I'm afraid to wake him. He has a temper and may kill me."

The English Captain's face flushed. He stood rigid and silent for several seconds. "Fine, I'll wake him."

"Do you want to get killed?" The first mate asked. The handful of sailors on the *Aud's* deck chuckled.

The English captain squared his shoulders and twisted his lips into a smile. "Allow me to show how a captain in the service of his majesty wakes your captain."

"You're welcome to try." The first mate stepped back from the lifelines.

The English ship moved closer to us and I heard the thump of several pairs of boots come on board. I heard the English captain shout, "Where is he, how do I get there?"

The footsteps got closer and I shut my curtains. They stood outside my door.

"Stop shouting, sir," the first mate said. "You don't want to upset him. He's the most dangerous commander in Norway.

A knock on the door turned into a fierce banging. I messed my hair and tried to appear like I'd just woke up. I shouted gibberish in a low German accent in hopes of proving our Norwegian origin.

I opened the door. "What the hell?" I did my best to look tired and upset.

"Good morning, sir." The English captain said. "Apologies for disturbing you." He held a rusty pistol in his left hand. He saluted me with his right hand, reaching up to his greasy cap. Six uniformed English soldiers stood behind him, fully armed.

I mustered in a harsh tone, "If you want to speak to me —allow me to get dressed." I slammed the door.

I stood behind the door and waited. Several long seconds of silence ticked by. The English captain said, "Are all captains in Norway such *bounders*?"

The first mate replied, "I don't know about all captains—but our captain has a reputation. Sir, would you mind waiting in the mess area for our captain?"

I heard a grumble of agreement through the door. The first mate had played his part well. I spent a half hour walking back and forth in my cabin. I laid back on my bunk and stretched out with my elbows behind my head. I thought about how to better play this dangerous game—the stakes were getting real.

The English captain had the authority to slaughter us if he felt we were a threat. What if the English party started to search the holds? What if they somehow found our stash of guns and ammunition for the Irish?

I pulled out the whiskey storage from under my bunk. I made it visible for anyone sitting on the couch to see. I opened my cabin door and shouted I was ready to receive the English. The captain came in and plopped on the couch. His attention went immediately to the six jugs of whiskey I had placed in the corner of the cabin.

My uniform coat, blade belt, and cutlass hung on the washstand. I tossed the towel I had dried my face with to the first mate and finished getting dressed. The English captain started with the usual inquiries, "Where were we from and where were we headed."

I told him we had engine trouble and were making for Tralee Bay to make repairs. He asked to look in the holds. I shrugged my shoulders and agreed. I hoped the men had taken this delay to re hide our contraband cargo. I told the first mate to have a few men take the seals off of the number 2 hold. The first mate nodded and gave me one of his shrewd winks.

I led the English captain down the holds for him to inspect. I followed behind the boarding party. I took silent deep breaths and tried to hide my anxiety. I fingered the trigger of my Browning gun in my pocket. I'd kill them if needed. I would do anything to protect my men and this mission.

The captain moved through the holds in a methodical manner. He searched every nook and cranny, but my men had enough time to conceal our weapons and ammunition. We left broken and damaged pieces of wood in the holds. When the English captain asked why, we told him it was from the previous storm that had damaged our boilers. I again made my point why we needed to make our repairs at Tralee Bay.

The English captain nodded his head and seemed satisfied with my answer. I asked him whether he wanted the lower holds opened. I put a stepping stool down and pointed in the direction of the dark and dank bottom holds.

He waved the stepping stool aside and said, "It's fine." He went on to tell me about how brutal the storm was here and how it nearly sunk his ship. He turned from the holds and I had him shepherded back to my cabin. I asked him if he wanted to see our papers. He nodded and I motioned for him to take a seat on the couch. I offered him a fat Havana and requested two cups of espresso from the steward.

When the steward arrived with the espresso, the English captain pushed it away. He was focused on the jugs of whiskey.

"Maybe a little whiskey then," I said and opened my arm to the corner of the room.

The captain's face lit up in a bright smile, "You're the man for me, sir." He stood up, slapped me on the shoulder and headed toward the whiskey jugs. He lifted the White Horse bottle and I handed him a tumbler.

I offered him a water bottle. He sneered and flicked his

wrist at it. "No water. I don't know how you drink whiskey in Norway—" He slugged down a full tumbler, wiped his lips with the back of his hand and refilled his glass. After a few more glasses, he pawed through our ship's papers and handed me a book to sign. I wrote, "Niels Larsen, skipper of the Norwegian liner Aud, with pit-props and piece merchandise from Christiania, for Cardiff and Genoa."

The English captain continued to refill his glass and drink. He went on to warn us about the detestable German submarines sinking every ship they found. And how the Irish rebels were stirring up trouble all over the coast.

I asked him for a couple of English newspapers and if he knew any recent war news. He shouted for one of his men to send over the newspapers from his personal cabin. While we waited, he continued spewing his hatred for our beloved Kaiser and the savage German murderers that started this war. My stomach knotted, flipped and soared. I bit down on my lip and nodded solemnly at his descriptions of the German devils.

The whiskey was getting to him and he slurred his speech. I closed my eyes and imagined smashing my fist into his fat mouth. I faked a smile and nodded my head. One of his men came to the cabin with a large stack of papers stuffed under his arm. I offered the man a whiskey and scanned over the headlines of the papers—any news of German victories or of the Irish rebellion.

Oh no. The headline of the second paper detailed the story of a handful of Sinn Fein rebels captured in Fenit. They were charged with treason and captured in Tralee Bay two days ago. The story went on to describe an Irish pilot also captured and charged. *Captured.* He was most definitely our pilot and those men were the Irish sent to accept the transfer of our cargo. Now what were we going to do?

I itched the side of my neck and handed the first mate the paper. I kept my thumb on the passage I'd just read. He nodded to me and a glimmer of disappointment dulled his face.

The English captain slapped me on the back and said in a soft, slurry, consoling tone, "Cap'n, don't you worry none about U-vessels. I'll watch out for you."

I nodded and thanked him.

"Your mate, said you were scared of the U-vessels," he continued, "I also understand you're to be hitched in a few months and you're ready to get back home."

I looked at the first mate and smiled. He shrugged his shoulders and gave me that shrewd wink.

The English captain refilled his glass, emptying the bottle of White Horse whiskey. "You don't stress. While you're here getting fixed up, I'll anchor at the cove entrance and make sure no U-vessels get in. I'd just ask for another bottle of that White Horse to take with me."

Damn. This was a disaster. "Thank you captain," I said, "I'm obliged to you." I reached under my bunk and pulled out another bottle of White Horse and handed it to him. What if Sir Roger tried to enter the bay in the German Submarine? He was bound to show up any second? Maybe he'd already been caught?

I made excuses of having to oversee the engine repairs to the captain and gave him another bottle of whiskey for his men. I thanked him for his help and bit back the urge to shoot him dead where he swayed in front of me like the drunken fool he was. We shook hands and I accompanied him to the gunwale of our ship. Once they'd left, I nodded to the first mate—he must've known we needed to talk.

I stood with him and the other officers and discussed our next plan. My men in the forecastle told me that the

English soldiers he'd brought aboard were dead drunk and could barely stand. So, if we dispatched the men, then what? We had no use for their ship. If we sank it, we'd bring more attention to us.

Due to the captures in the Tralee area, it was most likely that the whole region was under military law. It would be pointless to try and make contact with the Sinn Feiners. We had no other options but to send the rest of our whiskey to the English ship. Maybe they'd drink themselves further into a black hole. We would leave early tomorrow morning. We would give this rendezvous with the Irish one more night. If by tomorrow we still had not made contact with our Irish target, we would need to make a new plan.

When our pontoon boat returned from bringing the English ship more of our whiskey, we heard voices echoing through the bay. It wasn't singing, more like an awful drunken hollering. *Live it up.* I closed the door behind me after I entered the bridge. The first mate handed me a picture he'd taken from my cabin. I smiled and snickered. I told him this picture of my life partner was actually my sister.

I returned to my cabin and plopped onto my bunk. Time to recover, gather thoughts and plan. It was late, almost 3 a.m. The English ship was plied with every bottle of whiskey we'd had on board. I didn't expect to speak or rendezvous with the Sin Feiners. That operation was now over and what a waste. We journeyed into a wasp's nest and would probably survive. A new plan dawned on me. I hopped out of my bunk and called the whole crew to the upper deck to inform them of my plan.

In the next few hours we would slip past the drunken English ship and get thirty miles into the Atlantic before the moon rose. I was convinced luck was on our side. We would get away. We could sell our cargo of arms and ammunition in Spain—only a day's sail. If not there, then in Mexico. We would then refit our ship with more weapons and men. From there we'd hunt and destroy English trading vessels in the Atlantic.

SURROUNDED IN THE ATLANTIC

We slipped past the sleeping English ship guarding the cove. Our plan to ply them with whiskey worked. We got a halfhearted wave from their lookout as we slid by. By early afternoon we were back in the Atlantic on our way to Spain.

Another ship was spotted approaching us from the north. She was too far away to see at this distance—even with binoculars. I waited. As she came in closer, my stomach dropped. A long, fully exposed gun came into view on her forecastle. To her starboard side was another large English patrol ship. Both ships changed course and headed toward us.

I ordered all hands to emergency stations and steam up for max throttle. The men moved to their stations in seconds. I heard the *knock knock* from the engine room, and I shouted, "Due west course." *Maybe outrun them.*

The flotilla banner at her pole head signified their course change to south-west. They were going to try and cut us off. We needed to get to full steam faster. I ordered all hands to the stokehold. The smaller English ship was getting closer. We needed more speed. I called down to the stokehold from the voice-pipe to encourage them to work faster. They worked like race horses and we started to get ahead of our pursuers.

The English cruisers increased their speed and got closer. We were no match for them. Their battery firearms came into view. They were aimed at us. The two ships were surrounding us. We were being led into a pincer. The smaller cruiser looked to assault us from the front while the other would block us in.

The lead cruiser hoisted a signal: *Stop without a moment's delay*.

I ordered all explosives on our steamer primed. I'd starboard the rudder and if we were going down, I'd make damn sure to take at least one of them with us. What if I ran us at max speed into the lead English cruiser? What if she got out of our way? And sank us with her guns?

We waited. The English captain stood on the deck of his ship and watched us. If I had any whiskey left, I'd have tossed it to him. Would that work again? We were in a standoff. *For the Kaiser*. I gave the order to prepare to explode the ship. We would charge them and go down in history as heroes. The German flag was made ready to hoist. The chief gunner waited with the wire to explode the ship.

As if the English cruiser knew our plan—they steamed ahead. They got a nautical mile ahead of us. We were still inside the scope of their firearms. The second ship repositioned behind us. We were outmaneuvered. Could we breakout?

I gave the helm to the first mate and went below. The stokers worked with courage. Shirts off and sweat pouring down their bodies. They gleamed in contrast to the radiant heat. They worked as fast as possible. But it was not enough.

The first mate's voice echoed down the voice pipe "Get more steam. The English are closing the gap."

The chief engineer saw me and said, "Skipper, if we go on like this—the boilers will blast. The steam is well past the red imprint."

I nodded. "We still have a chance. Work your men as if the devil is snapping at their heels. Because he is."

The chief engineer saluted and twisted on his heel. He shouted, cursed and encouraged the men to work harder and faster. The first mate shouted down the voice tube for my presence on the bridge. I climbed out of the stoke hold, through the passageways and up the steps—two at a time. A third ship had joined the pursuit. We would be overwhelmed soon. Our speed had slowed to thirteen knots.

We were in the open Atlantic. Our Norwegian banner flew. I'd made it known to the drunken captain in the Tralee Bay that we were headed for Cardiff and then Italy. The English had no reason to destroy us. They had nothing against us. Why not keep up our appearances? No need to give these English warships any reason to be suspicious. We'd continue on our current course and convince the English we were no threat. Or we would kill as many of them as we could before going down.

FOLLOW US TO QUEENSTOWN

A hard north wind blew. The waves foamed and the current was in our favor. I called down to the chief engineer to rest the boilers and men. The three English cruisers surrounded and accompanied us but kept their distance. Another ship off the port bow appeared. A Norwegian tramp steamer. Just like us. Maybe she was the real *Aud*?

For ninety minutes we continued on. Like we were part of the English flotilla. We slinked our way into the Atlantic. How long could this last? The weather was clear and warm. No hope of a fog. Still over four hours of daylight left, and I wished for dusk. Was that our only hope of escape?

We planned for the unforeseeable future. We put the finishing touches on our dummy guns. The crew was in high spirits. They joked and talked about how much they looked forward to the prospect of sinking enemy merchant ships.

As 6 p.m. approached a cloud of smoke filled the south-western sky. She was a steamer with two chimneys. As she got closer, we identified the mastheads, the spotting top and the wireless masts. No mistaking it—another English warship. We calculated her speed at twenty knots. If we tried to flee, she could overtake us in less than an hour. If she didn't fire at us first. Remain calm and keep a clear head. This was our only choice—along with a little cunning.

The warship came on at her top speed. When her upper works were visible, we identified her as an English auxiliary cruiser. I reduced our speed to half. I again gave the order to prepare the ship for self-destruction and had everything put in its place. I ordered all our suspicious materials put back into the holds and hidden. We were back to acting like our old tramp steamer days.

No doubt this cruiser was called in from the wireless ship. We would be thoroughly examined. If we were lucky enough to survive another English captain and search, we'd surely be taken to the nearest port. Our cargo would be unloaded, and our ruse exposed. I won't let that happen. I'll take as many of these damn Englishmen with me as I blow up this ship.

The newest cruiser closed in on our port side. We were now pinned in on all four sides. Her four 5-inch guns trained on us. She zigzagged around us for ten minutes. If she would only get closer, I could sink her with us—just a little closer. Her crew was on deck. Armed with machine guns and staring at us like the curious creatures we were. We continued forward at our slow pace. If only I could breakout and steam east.

We kept this up until the sun finally set. It cast a dazzling reflection on the water, making it painful to scan the skyline. Once the sun disappeared behind the horizon on the starboard bow, a fifth ship came into view. What the hell. All five of them heavy English cruisers. We were trapped in the channel. Surrounded in all directions with no way out.

The English cruisers had modern, well-armed guns. Aside from our fake wooden cannons and small arms, we had nothing to fight with. Still, the so-called heroes of the sea must have expected a torpedo from us at any moment. They kept their distance and moved in a zigzag pattern around us. I wanted to laugh in their faces.

We continued on our course at half speed. Maybe this was an honor guard. Finally, just after seven o'clock, the cruiser on our port side, the *Bluebell* signaled for us to stop. The other ships kept their distance. Their guns aimed at us. Our dog barked and growled on the forecastle at the English cruiser as she got closer. Other signals came: *What is your cargo? Where are you from? Where are you bound?*

I could stick to the plan and tell them about Cardiff. But we were so far off course. Would they believe me? What about Genoa or Naples? We still had several door and window frames with this address. We needed more time. Could we slip away in the dark? I told the signalman to break the halyard when hoisting our next signal. Any delay would help. Maybe a U boat would come to our aid?

The English couldn't expect a tramp steamer to have a spare halyard on board. But we hung out one flag after the other to show the English we were trying to communicate with them. We kept this up for another fifteen minutes. After a pause, the *Bluebell* used her searchlights to communicate with the other cruisers. A constant crackling echoed over the water. This must mean she also used her wireless to communicate with the other ships. The signals were all going to the fifth cruiser off our starboard side. She must have the flotilla commander on board.

The *Bluebell* signaled us to proceed. Impossible. I don't understand. Was this another trick or trap? I was preparing for any possibility—but not this. Were we allowed to leave scot-free? I didn't hesitate. I ordered the first mate to set an easterly course and increase speed to full. Did we fool the English again? Did they believe we were the Norwegian *Aud*? How long could our luck continue to hold out? Something didn't sit right with me.

The English ships laid to our stern like a swarm of locusts. It looked like a war council. Were they reevaluating their foolish decision? I called down the voice-pipe to increase speed to maximum. At eight bells, the swarm of English cruisers increased speed and came at us like a pack of hounds.

The lead cruiser gave that familiar signal: Stop immediately. I ordered the *Aud* to stop and shut down her engines. I had no other choice If we didn't stop they might have engaged us. We waited for five long minutes. My nerves were getting jittery. The *Bluebell* again approached us. I signaled to ask why we were ordered to stop.

She didn't answer. At one-hundred and fifty yards off she lowered a cutter. Two officers and a dozen armed sailors. The English prize crew at last. We could capture and kill them if necessary. We'd have some success out of this failed mission. The first mate pointed and shouted, "Look out. Prize crew away." The men cheered. We had planned for this and everyone knew their part. We had a chance to at last—do something.

The English cutter got spooked and turned back to the *Bluebell*. Was it because of the repaired steam winch making an awful racket or the empty tin floating in the water confused as a periscope? In minutes we heard engine room telegraphs clang and the flotilla took off like they'd been struck by lightning.

How long was this cat-and-mouse game going to last? I signaled to the *Bluebell* for permission to proceed. I was told to wait. The cruisers cautiously approached, and I signaled them to ask: *Why wait?*

They replied: *Follow me to Queenstown, course south 63 east.*

A chill ran through me. They must have figured us out. We were finished. If only the prize crew would have come on board as planned. We could have dealt with them and taken some small victory from this mission. The heavily armed cruisers blocked our path on all sides again. We couldn't outrun them. Even in this new thick mist and pitch black night—we were trapped.

I answered back to their signal: *Don't understand.* All I could do now was delay and frustrate them, so they'd send the prize crew back to our ship. The *Bluebell* kept sending the same signal in different ways to make sure we understood. We looked like incompetent fools not being able to comprehend their signals.

The *Bluebell* tugged on their signal halyards and altered their course. Their flags blew in the wind. We continued our ruse. How much longer until the English figure out we were making a fool of them. The *Bluebell* came so close to us that even a half blind person could read their message. I shook my head and held up my signal book. The *Bluebell* captain threw up his hands and pointed at the flag again. We were now only fifty yards from their ship. A little closer and we could take them with us in an explosion.

Our delay tactics were working. Night came on and it was now truly difficult to read the signals. A man with a megaphone came out on their deck. I jumped out with my megaphone and said, "Can I lower the ladder for the prize crew?"

Maybe my enthusiasm spooked him, or he got new orders, but he made it clear my friendly invitation failed and they did not intend to send a prize crew. Our situation was grim. We were hemmed in by the other cruisers. Their guns aimed at us. Surely they'd fire at us if we tried anything. We'd be destroyed and with the distance the other cruisers kept from us—we would perish alone.

A petite lieutenant stood on the signaling bridge. He had the largest megaphone I'd ever seen and shouted over and over: *Follow me to Queenstown, south sixty-three east.* What could we do now? I was tired of playing the fool. The *Bluebell* captain seemed like he was losing his patience. He yanked the megaphone from the lieutenant and with a flurry of hand gestures, shouted orders.

The *Bluebell* changed course and crossed over our port side. A flash. *Boom.* A shell soared over our bow. They repositioned their guns. It was clear the next shell would not be fired over our bow—but into the bridge. This game was over. I hurried out onto the deck and waved my arms. I cupped my hands to my mouth and shouted, "full speed ahead, south, 63 east."

The English captain stood with his arms crossed and gave a curt nod. I told the chief engineer through the voice tube that we were not to exceed a speed of five knots under any circumstances.

At our current pace, we'd reach Queenstown by 10 a.m. We had to follow the cruiser. I couldn't think of any other option to resist. The other English cruisers were scattered around us. We had a spectacular escort. The wind changed direction to NNW and then died. The last few clouds disappeared and with it our last chance of escape.

The *Bluebell* signaled us with her lamp. She was not pleased with our slow speed. The more she signaled us, the more I reduced our speed. We used a tiny paraffin lamp and made the Morse dots and dashes by holding a hand in front.

I can only imagine how much this infuriated the English captain.

They kept signaling: *Faster, move faster.*

I replied: *Don't understand* and afterward I sent: *Impossible.*

Bluebell: *Why?*

Aud: *Engine malfunction.*

Several minutes passed with no response. I'm sure they had a heated discussion on how to make us move faster. The next message was to the point: *Speed up immediately. Or we shall make you.* Apart from being rude and harsh, what could they really do?

All this effort to get us to the nearest port. Would they fire on us for being slow? Maybe they'd get frustrated and send a prize crew. This was our best-case scenario at the moment. I sent a message to the English that this was our top speed due to engine malfunction and invited them to board and see for themselves.

Again, the English refused. They must have accepted their fate because we received no more signals from them. We continued our crawl behind them. They zigzagged to the left and right. Did they expect us to fire a torpedo at them? If only we had a torpedo.

THE AUD'S DESTRUCTION

At midnight, our squadron of escort cruisers departed on a due west course. This left only the *Bluebell.* She was behind us. The clear night made our current situation easy to see. Toward the north, lights of other vessels shone through every now and then. If only a German submarine could help us. The moon lit the water in front of us. Our fate was only a few hours away.

I gathered the crew on the deck. I made it clear to the men that we had failed in our mission. If no help arrives by morning, we were duty bound to destroy the *Aud*. We could not let her fall into enemy hands. The men stood in solemn agreement. They knew the risks. After a few minutes, the chief engineer and the first mate started a long string of curses directed at the English. I allowed myself a smile. But the reality of our situation was that we were helpless in the claws of the enemy.

I ordered the burning of all secret documents. We dumped into the ocean any valuables we couldn't burn. In case our explosion wasn't effective, we could leave no clues for the enemy. I thought about unloading the machine guns meant for the Irish and firing at our heavily armed enemy. My crew was not trained in their use and we ran the chance of failing to destroy the *Aud.*

I inspected our ship with the first mate. I was satisfied that our explosive precautions were all in place. I examined every detonator, explosive charge and incendiary bomb. Our German naval flag was ready to hoist on my signal. I wanted to wait for the right opportunity to torch our ship. Maybe another cruiser will get close. I do not want to die alone and in vain.

The moon was high and clear. The night was quiet, and stars twinkled without a wisp of clouds to block their sparkling light. The ocean was a glass-like smooth. Only a gentle breeze unsettled her surface. Under normal conditions, I couldn't have asked for anything better than this.

Boat lights off the far north appeared. Other boats without lights crossed our course. Some of them came close enough to see their crew. Maybe even close enough to take them with us to hell. The majority were destroyers and English watch boats. They steamed without lights in fear of our German submarines that owned the sea. If only we could contact a U boat and tell them our position. They could destroy or distract the *Bluebell* and we could get away.

We continued on, mile after mile. A long, dim strip that looked like a low-lying cloud bank revealed the coast. We were closing in on Queenstown harbor. It was time to choose the spot of our destruction. I searched the charts for where we could do the most damage with our explosion.

Sunrise peeked over the horizon. The *Bluebell* modified her course toward the coast. "It's a perfect day to die, sir." The first mate said behind me. "Have you decided where?"

I turned, shook my head and put my hand on his shoulder. "Easter Sunday is just as good a day as any other."

The other ships from our escort had returned. They hemmed us in but still kept their distance. They were curious about what we were doing. I had ordered the men to wear their German uniforms under the Norwegian outfits. When I gave them the signal, they would shed their calfskin coats and be in proper colors.

We rounded the passageway and Cookroom Lighthouse came into view. Only fifteen more minutes until we arrive. Could we get close enough to a moored warship and take her with us? It was time to make a decision. No need to sacrifice every man on board. I asked for three volunteers to stay with me to explode the *Aud*. One man to raise the German colors, the others to coordinate the blast and ensure our destruction.

The men in near unison shouted, “No. We will stay till the end.” These were the bravest men I'd ever known and will be forever grateful for their fearless loyalty.

I signaled the *Bluebell* and asked them: *Where were we to grapple?*

They replied with: *Anticipate further requests.*

It was time. Let's see if they could anticipate this. The first mate tapped me on the shoulder and pointed out a large English liner moving fast on a crossing course. A brilliant plan dawned on me.

“Ten points to Port,” I called to the quarter master. “Keep her steady.” The *Aud* creaked and moaned and changed her course. “All hands to quarters. Prepare to hoist colors.” The men jumped to action. We were inside eight-hundred yards of the English liner. The liner changed her course to hard a-starboard. She passed us with a wide berth.

Had our luck finally run out? The lighthouse was less than two hundred yards in front of us. I searched for any sign of a periscope in the water. Nothing. Not even a preserved meat tin that looked like a periscope. It was time to accept our fate.

"All prepared," I shouted to the men. Gathered and waiting for my signal.

"Every single sailor is ready and able to do their duty, captain." The first mate replied after confirmation from the voice tube. I gave the signal.

The *Aud* jerked hard to port and laid in the center of the channel. The German naval ensign was hoisted. The crew tossed their Norwegian coats over the side of the ship. We cheered as loud as we could for the Kaiser. A muted blast. The men fell to their stomachs on the deck. The *Aud* shuddered from stem to stern. Pillars and splinters flew in all directions followed by a haze of filthy dark smoke. Flames burst from the chart house and forecastle.

I pulled myself to my feet. I shouted, "All hands to the pontoons." The *Aud* was going down. But I could still save my men from a watery grave before the ammunition in the holds exploded.

The port side pontoon pushed off under the direction of the first mate. The starboard pontoon was stuck. The flames were getting closer. Hotter. The helmsman cut the painter line with a hatchet. I followed my men and was the last into the pontoon. The bow was low in the water and sinking slowly.

"All away," I said in the calmest voice I could muster.

"Ay, ay, sir." The men on the pontoon responded.

The other pontoon boat joined us as we made a desperate attempt to escape the sinking *Aud*. Another savage blast ignited amidships. More followed with thick billows of sulfurous smoke. These must be the weapons exploding into flames. A gun fired. The *Bluebell* fired at the *Aud*. I couldn't see where the shell struck through the flames. The cruisers turned toward our pontoons. Would they attack us? I ordered my men to raise a white banner from each pontoon. Would the English disregard global law and slaughter us here?

The bow of the Aud snapped and submerged. Oil and debris littered the area around our former ship. No further blasts. I watched the sea fill into the enormous gap in the ship's side. The water surged in and she bobbed. In seconds, the poles tottered, and the stern shot down into the channel with a giant *clang* and *crack*.

I stood up in the pontoon and stared at the empty ocean where the Aud had been only seconds ago. Our *Libau* and then *Aud* was gone.

THE LAWS OF WAR

I stood and faced the *Bluebell.* I waved the white banner and shouted, "German sailors. We demand confirmation of our surrender."

No answer. I ordered the men to row our pontoon closer to the English ship. Would they accept our surrender? Would they fire a volley into us once we got closer? It seemed as if every English sailor on the cruiser had a weapon pointed at us. A wave of dread washed over me. Did they think we were going to sink their cruiser with our pontoons?

The hodge-podge of armed men glared at us. Unwashed, unshaven sailors and soldiers with toned shirts. Even the captain wore hued jeans and a dull uniform coat. The men without rifles had edged weapons at the ready. Sabers, cutlasses, and other weapons looked like they were dug up from the 18th century.

The hatred on their faces was clear. We would be treated with the same contempt that the English regarded most German military men. A short lieutenant stepped forward and gestured for our pontoon to row aft. A ladder lowered for only me to board the *Bluebell*. After I pulled myself on their deck, a nervous looking six men with rifles enclosed around me. A searchlight shone on me from the upper deck. This was ridiculous. I am an enemy officer captured in war and I must be treated with respect. How can the English just disregard the rules of war?

The lieutenant barked an order in a stifled voice. The six armed men in a crescent around me took a step closer and prepared to fire. Other crew members had gathered on the deck. It was turning into a mob. I shut my eyes and took a deep breath. I was serenaded by shouts of "Shoot the German pig" and "Kill the German dog." Was this how I would meet my end? Cut down on an English ship like a common criminal? And what would happen to my men? Would they be treated the same?

I made a motion to step toward the lieutenant. The cold barrel of a rifle jarred into my chest. The lieutenant barked another order to his men, and they shouldered their weapons. The group grew louder and more angry. Shouts of "Hang the pirates" and other jeers continued with whistles, clapping and deck stomping.

I looked over my shoulder at my men in the pontoons. I shook my head at the first mate and hoped he understood my meaning of stay calm and do nothing. I needed to diffuse this situation and get honorable terms. In my best English I said, "take me to the captain. We are German sailors and per global law will be treated as such." I glared at the little lieutenant.

He hesitated. He looked uncertain of what to do. He looked at me for a long second, then to his men as if looking for counsel. I thought of the Baralong incident. A global scandal that dishonored the English Navy. Maybe this would save us. I summoned my courage and shouted, "We are legitimate prisoners of war. Unless you plan to commit another war crime and shoot us down like the Baralong did to the surrendering German U-boat sailors."

This may have worked. The sailors surrounding me took a step back and the taunting shouts stopped.

I continued, "If you have no honor then do what you must do. Just know that for every innocent German prisoner you murder—two English will be shot. I have nothing more to say to you."

An English sailor rushed up to the lieutenant and whispered in his ear. He nodded and frowned at me. He ordered the men from the pontoons taken aboard. We were held at gunpoint on the center deck of the English cruiser. The sailors searched us. The frustration on their faces was clear when they failed to find anything useful.

A sailor asked the men if they had weapons hidden. The helmsman shouted, "yes." He pointed to his large left boot. An English sailor felt down his leg, while two others held his arms. They pulled out a huge German frankfurter. This caused a hearty laughter from my men until the English soldier slammed the butt of his rifle into the helmsman's face.

We were taken below, and I was isolated from my men. I was questioned by several officers. The little lieutenant assured me in a regretful tone that we would be treated as prisoners of war. The engine of the *Bluebell* started. We must be on our way into Queenstown. I was brought out on deck and escorted to the *Adventure*. I was marched at rifle point with my men in a line behind me. Onboard the *Adventure*, I was again separated from my men.

Given better food and treated with consideration and respect. While there was no compassion, I was told our failed mission to Ireland was a "shrewd attempt." After a whole day of being questioned, I was taken to Spike Island in the harbor. I was desperate for any news of our mission or the war. The English refused to answer any questions. Had the Irish rebellion started? Were they winning? Where was Sir Roger Casement?

Our escorts got larger and more English officers joined in the questioning fray. After several more hours I was taken to a cell inside the harbor fortification. Guards lined the hallways. A small window shaded by iron bars lit the cell. Except for a rusty iron bed stand and a flimsy table, there were no furnishings. A man dressed as a priest came to my cell. Was this my end?

The priest was an Irish patriot and eager to help. While he couldn't help with my escape or that of my crew. He did have news. The Irish had risen. On Easter Sunday they'd taken Dublin from the English overlords. Other parts of Ireland were throwing off their shackles as well. I learned Sir Roger had been captured by the English. He snuck in a recent paper. It read that a German ship had attempted to land arms and weapons for Irish rebels was sunk in Queenstown harbor. Sunk by English guns. It stated that Sir Roger was a spy for the German war effort. The English had now thoroughly understood our business. But where did they learn this? Not from me. Was there a spy? We were relegated to nothing more than crew members under the direction of Sir Roger. English fools.

We were interrupted and I was taken back to the *Bluebell*. Why couldn't they make up their mind what to do with me? I spent the next two days on the cruiser under the watchful eye of the little lieutenant. In my boredom I was able to make comparisons between the conditions on the two ships. On the *Adventure*, it was immaculate. The men I came into contact with were careful and official. The *Bluebell* was the most uncouth and unsavory ship I'd ever had the misfortune of spending time on.

I was offered a glass of whiskey several times during my captivity. The crew was appalled when I refused and instead asked for an espresso. A beverage that was beneath these honorable men. Even though they knew our true mission, I continued my web of lies. I told them the arms and ammunition we carried were for our troops in Africa. I spun a story about sneaking through the English barricade to set up a trade assault route. The frustration on each officers face knowing that they lost the chance to claim the Aud as a prize before she was sunk—thrilled me.

The next day the *Bluebell* set out to sea. I wasn't told our destination and kept in the little lieutenants quarters. A guard came in and screwed down a covering over the porthole—no more ocean view. I guessed this must be the spot we sunk the *Aud*.

We tacked through the harbor for what seemed like hours. Maybe I'd chosen the right spot to sink her. I could only hope I disrupted their shipping. The cruiser picked up speed. I could feel us out on the open ocean. Where were they taking me?

SHOT IN THE TOWER

Early the next morning I was escorted off the *Bluebell* by a half dozen marines. I stood on the rainy southwest shore of England. My stomach growled as I was pushed onto a train. Over the next eighteen hours, I was given two pieces of bread—no spread and a little water. The marines wouldn't reveal our destination. When we stopped, men came to our window and pounded on it. They were out for blood.

A larger mob met us at every station. Was this were I'd meet my end? Ripped apart by an angry mob in England. The marines tried to calm the crowd. I heard them say that I was going to the tower of London and I would be shot.

We arrived at our destination after midnight. It was total darkness. The lights must have been dampened in fear of a Zeppelin strike. I was marched by the crew of marines through dim roads to an enormous structure. It was only me. What had happened to my men? I was led up two winding stairways in the dark. A cell was waiting, open to receive me. The marines shoved me in and turned a giant key in the lock. I was alone.

* * *

THE NEXT MORNING an English admiral came to visit. I saluted after he entered. The admiral gave a disgusted look. He didn't return my salute, not even with his stick. *Rude.* He asked the same questions that dozens of others asked about our adventures. I kept my answers as short and misleading as possible. He left not long after with a sneer and a shrug.

Days passed and I was left to myself. The interrogations stopped. The only human contact was the guard opening my cell to slide a plate of cold food inside. He must also be making sure I hadn't hanged myself. I spent my time pondering. How would I escape? It was my duty as a German officer to resist. I had no options. Trapped and at the mercy of my English captors.

What was going on outside of here? What would happen to me? My men? I tapped on the iron bars. The guards refused to answer any of my questions. A feeling of doom shuttered through me.

I woke up the next morning to find my clothes—uniform, shoes, what I'd taken off to sleep was missing. I thumped the cell door and demanded an answer from the guard. He walked over dragging his wooden club against the bars making a clinking noise as he got closer. Was he trying to intimidate me?

"We took them off to get sewn back up." The guard smiled. "I heard the tailor found plenty a Danish banknote hidden in your clothes. That ain't gonna look to good for you—Hun."

I had no reply. This was bad karma and now I lost my ability to bribe guards. My clean and resewn clothes were flung into my cell. Another officer I hadn't seen yet stood outside of my cell and took me to the first floor. I passed a cell full of my men. I only took a quick glance as I shuffled past, but they seemed healthy. The English officer shoved me forward. Where the hell was he taking me?

Once outside, I saw we were in Chatham. We headed back to the train station. A crowd had gathered, but they were much calmer than the angry mob on the way here from the coast. We boarded a train for London. I felt like a lamb taken to slaughter.

I stood outside Scotland Yard. The wind whipped through me to my bones. My teeth chattered. I was brought inside and no time was wasted presenting me to the Admiralty. The room was crowded with General Staff officials, Naval officers, and even the London police commissioner. I declined their offer for a translator. My English was good enough for this.

They wanted to know where the German fleet was. *Ha!* Even if I knew, I'd never tell them. I made it clear that I would not speak a word that would compromise any German war interests. This irritated them and I hid a smile.

The English outlined our plan. They knew everything in precise detail. How was it possible? Who was the spy? The English would give no information. I asked about Sir Roger. I didn't confirm any of their information, but by the look on my face, they got their answer. They continued asking the same questions. I refused to answer them until they answered my questions about Sir Roger.

After a muffled deliberation, the main English investigator sat across from me in a chair. He looked at me for a long second in silence. Was he trying to intimidate me? Did he think I would gush information? I stared back and put my chained wrists on the table. I cocked my head to the side and waited for him to speak.

"Sir Roger Casement is being held in a cell here." The

investigator said. "You'll join him on the gallows soon enough. After you answer my questions."

Did Sir Roger sell us out? Was this a feint to get me to talk? I believed he was here—if he was even captured. I had to hold myself together. "I want to speak to him," I said. "Then, I'll give you the answers you're looking for." Feign against feign. Let's see how he likes this game now.

In my gut I believed Sir Roger was being held here. If Sir Roger was the spy and he had sold us out—we were finished. The investigator paused and looked over his shoulder. The long awkward pause continued for several seconds. They continued to ask questions about our mission and orders. I refused to speak. The investigator's tone of voice got louder and he gripped the edges of the wooden table like a vise.

He stood up, his chair slid back, making a loud scratching noise. He leaned in to my face. His breath smelled like tobacco. "You exploded your ship after being taken prisoner. You will be sentenced to death." The corners of his mouth rose in an uneven smile, revealing stained yellow teeth.

I shook my head, "Lies. Unless you plan to evade universal law and murder me."

The investigator spun around and stormed out of the room. I was taken to another room and shoved into a chair. Two English police stood silently on either side of me. What now? They couldn't execute me? Could they? The English would have to prove a gross infringement of universal law. This was nonsense. A ploy to scare me. An interrogation technique to get me to betray my country. When I followed the *Bluebell* to Queenstown, I was no way a detainee. I was a neutral complying with their order, because there was no other course available. But would the English see it that way?

Would the English try to prove we broke global law by using the Norwegian banner? They could argue we acted in a dishonorable manner and should be treated like privateers —hanged or shot.

The next few days I was kept in isolation. What would happen to us? The guards were tight lipped and from the muffled conversation and sidelong glances an eerie feeling crept over me.

At night the lights flickered, and the walls shook. The sirens blared for hours. Screams of the "Zepps are coming" echoed through the walls. I pulled my knees to my chest and tightened the blanket around my shoulders. Maybe the Zeppelins would bomb the English into submission. My hope faded. The nighttime raids cheered my spirits. I accepted whatever was to come.

* * *

MORE DAYS PASSED. A marine escort came for me one morning. I stopped counting days. They rolled into each other now. I was being transferred to a POW camp. The marine officer told me my men had also been transferred there the previous day. After a long train ride to Derby, I was at Castle Donington. I was to be held at Donington Hall Camp as a prisoner of war.

So it was true. Only a threat to convince me to betray my country. They failed, and I endured. And now I was safe, my men were safe—held in a prison camp—but not executed as common criminals.

My shackles were undone and I was led into a series of iron doors. Each one clanked and shut with a powerful clang. I was released into the courtyard to the applause of my men. The first mate was the first to greet me.

"Glad to see you made it, sir," he said. "We've become quite the sensation here." He handed me a newspaper with the headline: *The Journey of the Aud-Norge.*

Our story had landed on the front page of the Times in London. Sir Roger had reached Tralee Bay after we'd left. The appearance of the U-boat had riled the drunken captain and crew guarding the cove. Sir Roger tried to flee and ran aground in a collapsible pontoon. He was surrounded and captured by the English. His capture hindered the Irish rebels. The failure to deliver vital war supplies doomed the Irish cause. They were short of rifles and ammunition. They had nothing to overwhelm the big English guns. This was a major cause of the failed six week Easter uprising.

Sir Roger was tried and condemned to be hanged. On August 3, while I sat in a Scotland Yard cell, Sir Roger's sentence was carried out. Sergeant Bailey—Sir Roger's devoted assistant—had double crossed him to save his own life.

MY ESCAPE ATTEMPT

My thoughts turned to escape. Every day was consumed with dreams of freedom. I yearned to rejoin the war effort and punish the English for declaring war on Germany. How would I escape from this camp?

According to universal law, the English could not charge us with the same war crimes as Sir Roger. I didn't trust the English and had no intention of waiting here to find out what kind of surprise they might invent. I would not share Sir Roger's fate. I had a duty to resist and escape.

Whenever I got an opportunity, I investigated my surroundings. I tried to get as close to the perimeters of the camp and find vulnerable spots. The security here was tight. This wasn't a prison for common criminals. Donington Hall was renowned for being the most secure wartime captive camp in England.

Since the escape of Commander Plüschow in July 1915, no other prisoner had escaped. Many tried, but with the war on, people were suspicious. Streets, railroad stations, and docks were watched with vigilance. There was also the problem of food. Without a food-card, there was no legal way to get food during the rationing.

I discussed the possibilities with my first mate. He had resigned himself to waiting out the war here. He argued that even if I could get out past the gate, I'd get no further. How much longer could this war last? I reminded him of his duty to resist. He agreed to follow me to the end. But maybe I'd be better off without him. I couldn't get all my men out of here. And if I did, would I be condemning them to death? No. I would escape alone. It was my duty as a German officer. My men had done their duty. But the burning question was how?

* * *

MONTHS PASSED. I was no closer to figuring out an escape. My men were transferred away to another prison. I needed to occupy my mind and avoid a psychological breakdown. I'd met new friends, captured German officers bold enough to attempt an escape. We spent our days thinking of ways to overcome our many challenges.

We needed cash. I had those banknotes sown into my clothes for times such as these. If we had cash, we could bribe the guards and get our needed supplies. We were searched on a regular basis and due to the secure nature of the camp, nearly everything useful to aid us in our escape was illegal. Cash, folding knives, even the smallest hammer —all banned. We were given metal tokens to use as camp currency. We had to give receipts for any purchases or trades.

How would we get non-military clothes and fake papers? If we had cash, we could bribe an English officer or one of the camp workers. They weren't too keen on taking our metal tokens—not that I even asked.

I had become a celebrity in the English press due to our adventures. I was viewed as like a "Sherlock Holmes" and the guards kept a close watch on me. I drew attention most places I went in the camp. The guards found it amusing and they would draw themselves up into attention and mock me with a salute, "Good morning Casement skipper" or "Post! Captain Spindler is coming."

Whenever a new English officer came to review the prisoners, the camp commandant would point to me, "That tall German is the man who brought Casement to Ireland." It became exhausting, I resisted the urge to tell them that I brought the weapons and a U-boat brought Sir Roger. After continued embarrassing comments, I wrote a letter to the English colonel in charge. I asked him to stop having his officers treat me like a zoo animal. He never answered me, but not long after the guards and camp officers never mentioned it again.

A rumor spread that in the basement of the clock tower was an escape tunnel leading into the nearby town of Castle Donington. It was supposed to be used by the camp officers and guards if the prison was attacked. Was this true? Did it matter? Now, I had hope. I had something to hold on to and think about. I could make a plan and if there really was a tunnel down there, I'd find it and use it as a means to make my escape.

I spent my time trying to think of creative ways to find this passageway. I weaseled my way into a job in the basement of the clock tower. For only a few hours a day I was allowed down there. Near the steps was a switchboard and an electric light kept on day and night. I managed to sneak in a small knife that I hid behind the steps in the basement.

I worked in shifts with another captive. One of us would search for the tunnel while the other watched the steps and for any guards. Our job was to remove the rubble from the basement. But our real job was to find the entry to the tunnel that would lead us to freedom.

* * *

WEEKS PASSED while we searched for our passage to freedom. I refused to give up hope. I would find a way out of here. The war needed me. With the faint glow of the electric light, I tapped on a divider and heard a hollow thud. Was this the opening? Did I find it? I tapped on the stone again. A deeper, emptier sound. This was it. Everything inside told me that I'd found the underground entry. I scratched a mark into the stone and hurried up the stairs. It was time to plan our next step.

The next morning as we went to the basement, I passed two locksmiths. Shock rushed through me and I couldn't move. Were we found out? I continued to the entryway behind the stairs in the basement. Locked. The pinnacle entryway that led to the passage was secured. But why? It didn't feel any different. How would I get into the clock tower passage?

Weeks passed with a guard placed on the stairs. They knew something—but what? We were never questioned or challenged. Did they discover a loose stone? Time to think of another way. I knew where the path was, I needed to find a way to access it.

The château chapel was twenty yards off from the clock tower. Maybe it had access to the entryway? That night in the darkness I snuck out to see for myself. The night was black. No stars, no moonlight, I felt my way along the sides of the walls and down the stairs into the chapel.

Once inside, I lit a match. The sulfur smell mixed the mildew made me hack up a mouthful of phlegm. The flicker of the match illuminated that I stood over a pole. I continued using matches as a guide until I stumbled into the final resting places of the long-dead Barons of Donington.

I continued to cough and hack like a dying man. I tried to cover my mouth before I brought the night watch down on me. Something dashed over my feet. *Rats.* I held my breath and lit another match. I glanced down and saw dozens of them scurrying away.

At least they weren't ghosts. I could deal with rats. But it was unusually cold down here. What if I lost my soul to a phantom trying to find my way out? I shook my head and steadied my nerves. *Focus. Find a way out.*

I came to an enormous stone divider. I felt the damp stones—the mortar was crumbled away. Was one of these stones the passage to the *passage*? Something told me I was in the right place. Maybe it was a ghost, or a rat. I jabbed a handful of used matches into the decaying mortar to mark my place. This had to be it. I needed more time to investigate. But now, back to bed before getting caught.

I found religion not soon after that. Any opportunity to get to the chapel and poke around in the daylight I found a way to take advantage of. I arranged a job where I brought in oak to the chapel for the builders to create a new room. For over two weeks I made progress sneaking down into the stones and digging out the mortar to find entry into the passage.

My plans were brought to a standstill by the failed escape attempt of a Naval Lieutenant. He had gotten outside of the spiked metal fence with a wooden board he'd made in secret. He'd spent five months creating a box like structure to protect him from the fence. Since it was hopeless to get any real lumber in this camp, he used the wood from discarded cigar boxes.

While his escape attempt was impressive, the guard was tripled. We were scrutinized much harder and our freedom of movement was restricted to open areas. This would set my escape back months. Our food was reduced because of the damage caused by our U-boats. I was hungry all the time. How was I going to stockpile food? I needed at least seven days' worth to stand any kind of chance. The English also suffered. Guards would offer to pay me for a bit of my bread because their rations were reduced.

The chapel and clock tower were now off limits and heavily guarded. Time to think of a new plan. The constant setbacks had gotten to me. I couldn't give up. I had to find a new way. A new plan. I offered my services as an orderly at the emergency clinic. I was trained in basic first aid. My English helped me build trust with the officers. The occasional question would arise: Do you ever think about trying to get away from here?

I'd make it a point to say how that was a dishonorable and ridiculous idea. Only a fool would consider such a plan, especially because of how dire the conditions had become with the war on.

I wrote a letter to the prize court in London. In detail, I described how without the Danish banknotes taken from me, I couldn't buy any clothes or more food. I requested that the choices to deprive me of my property be re-examined. Less than two weeks later, all the banknotes taken from me in the Tower of London were returned. I spread the bills out on my bed. My mind surged with possibilities. Could I find a way out of here after all?

I never gave up hope for my escape. Different ideas swam through my head and I never stopped thinking about it. I created a bouncing post constructed from brush handles. I could use it to hop over the spiked metal perimeter? On its first trial run it snapped in half. I tried again. With another shaft that also broke on the first try. A long, thick tree branch sat on top on the fence. What if I could get some rope and somehow get it around that branch—and climb out? The next day the guards cut that branch and trimmed back the tree.

A small car consistently came to camp over the last few weeks. I approached the driver and tried to make small talk. He was open to making cash and before long we agreed that he'd sneak me out of camp in the back of his car for £500.

The problem was I didn't have the money. Not all of it, anyway. I could raise some of it now and after the war I could repay him the rest. The Englishman reluctantly agreed—I sensed a desperation about the man. We settled on the day and hour. It was really going to happen. I would have a chance to make my escape.

* * *

THREE NIGHTS LATER, I crept into the yard close to the carport. I waited. Thirty minutes, sixty minutes. Did he make a fool out of me? I turned to slink back to my bunk when headlights lit up the carport in the yard. The car approached, I recognized the driver—but he had two English officers with him, Was I betrayed?

I crawled along the divider into the darkest corner of the carport. My heart pounded in my chest. I closed my eyes. All

I heard was *thump, thump, thump* the driver swiveled his head. He was looking for something—or someone. He had a nervous expression on his face. The two English officers hopped out of the car and walked to the commandant's office. The driver called the closest guard over and told him he needed petrol. Once the guard had gotten far enough away and the coast was clear, I showed myself to him.

The driver held his palm to my chest, "I'm gambling a ten year prison sentence helping you," he said.

I nodded. I stepped to his side and looked over my shoulder. He stood in my way again.

"This is no joke," he continued. "I want all the money now. How do I know I'll get paid, once yer out of here. Not worth the risk."

I stood over him by four inches. I looked down and whispered, "not our deal. We made a—"

"I don't care. Money now or no deal." He held out his palm, "hurry up and decide, officers be back soon."

Double crossing English bastard. I don't have it even if I wanted to give it to him. What if I broke his neck and took the car? How far could I get? Would I get hunted down and shot like an animal? The sound of crunching gravel pulled me from my dilemma. The guard. I had no option. I slunk away back to my bunk. How could I be such a fool to trust him? Now what would I do?

TOMMIES IN THE NEIGHBORHOOD

Constant failure and disappointment wore on my nerves. These strategies were never going to succeed. I needed to come up with something new, innovative, something no one had dared to try before. But what?

I needed a bigger plan. What was the goal of escaping this camp? To get trapped and ambushed in the English countryside. To truly escape—I must flee England. Just one problem, the North Sea, that body of water blocking my way home. How was I supposed to overcome that?

I'd need a boat or pontoon to take me to Germany. The English coast was tightly guarded and watched. Even before news of an escape. Could I stroll up and steal a boat? Bargain for one? Murder a fisherman and take his? I ruled out no options.

The quickest way to get home was via air. This was by far the best way to escape England. This idea presented two problems. First, I'd need to find an aerodrome near Donington Hall. Second, I'd need a pilot. I've never even sat in a plane. I would find a way. I could work out the details in due course. What was important was that I settled on a plan. Now, how to make it work?

I was able to get my hands on a Meyer's Encyclopedia. I found that the closest aerodrome to Donington was in Nottingham. To reach Ostend in Belgium was roughly three hundred kilometers. Less than two hours of air travel. If I ran out of fuel, I could ditch in the North Sea and hope for a U-boat rescue.

Fuel was even more highly guarded than the ports and boats. I could find it somewhere near the aerodrome. I remember from my train travels through the country that the flying ground at Hendon, one of the biggest in England, was unguarded.

This idea stuck with me for weeks. I obsessed over it. I was never able to let myself rest. I would be free soon and not just lost in the English countryside waiting to be caught —but free and home in Germany. I would be a hero.

* * *

I NEEDED A PILOT. Not just any pilot, one that could operate one of the cutting edge British planes. New prisoners arrived daily. Most were caught after they'd just joined the war and had little experience flying. I needed an expert pilot. One who had the skills to get us out of this damned country.

I paid more attention to the planes that flew over our camp. I noticed they always flew over the camp in a northern direction. Where were they headed exactly? An English officer I'd become friendly with from the emergency clinic gave me an old novel. It had maps outside of Donington and of the southern parts of England. It even showed a part of the North Sea and into Belgium.

Any arriving prisoners that passed through Nottingham on their way here were of great interest to me. The new detainees had all heard of the "Casement captain," they were eager to help mc and hear the story of how we exploded the *Aud* in Queenstown Harbor.

From these men, I learned that an aerodrome was being built close to the railway station. Less than eight kilometers from here. The first two hangers had been built and the third was near completed. My interviews with these men proved it could be a major biplane operational base.

My luck was back. I even got information that only one watchman guarded the unfinished aerodrome. Even if there were two guards, I could overpower them and tie them up before any alert was sounded.

I'd used some of my remaining money to buy cigarettes. I offered them to camp workers in the hope of making friends. One older Englishman was chatty. We talked about the planes that flew over us every day. How could I get more information on the exact aerodrome location?

I asked him about the British pilot that crashed a few days ago. I pointed in a direction I knew to have no aerodrome. The old man shook his head. No pilot crashed there, because there was no flight path or aerodrome there. He then confirmed for me the location of the closest aerodrome —just outside of Nottingham. I passed him a handful of cigarettes and told him he was mistaken. There couldn't be an aerodrome there. The old man swiped the cigarettes from my hand and turned away.

The next day I was given a large, detailed cycling map of the area. These cigarette bribes had worked wonders. I slipped the map into my back pocket and made excuses to leave.

The prison camp was getting crowded. New German

POWs arrived daily. A new fence was built around the old one. More guard boxes constructed. Newer, stricter rules enforced. It was as if they knew I was planning my escape.

I kept up my strategy of playing "the beaten man." I avoided games and physical activity. I hung on the edges of the tennis court and watched, plotted, and planned my next move. One afternoon, there was a downpour. The rain ran off the tennis courts and softened the surrounding ground, making a ravine. Big enough for two men to lie in and hide.

* * *

FLIGHT LIEUTENANT WINKELMANN arrived at the camp. He'd been shot down on the Western front. Young, full of fight and energy, he introduced himself to me as W. He told me my exploits with the *Aud* were known throughout Germany —I was a national hero. We became friends and I told him about my escape plans. W didn't hesitate. It seemed he wanted out of this prison more than even I did.

He knew about the cutting edge British planes. He'd often flown captured planes behind the lines. He also spoke English. This was going to work. With more enthusiasm than I'd had since my capture, we made our plans.

I went to the camp medical officers and told them I had "mental meltdown" and needed to remain in bed. No communication was passed to the other guards. At the evening prisoner count. "Where is Captain Spindler?" boomed through the night.

I was assigned to see a medical specialist. He would make the final decision on my condition. As I walked to his office, I passed the tennis courts. The channel had grown larger, tall grass on the edge camouflaged it. Almost large enough to hide W and me.

How would I fool this doctor? I practiced twitching and chain-smoked packs of cigarettes. He didn't know what to think of it and said he'd visit me in my bed tomorrow. The chain smoking made my heart beat irregular and I felt sick. When he arrived, it was a perfect storm of me playing the part. He listened to my chest and recommended milk, bread rolls, and prescribed medication.

He made his report that I was sick. The guards stopped asking for me at the night count. I often covered my head with a blanket to pretend I couldn't take the glare of the electric lamp. For the first week, the guard would lift the cover and look at my face.

After that week, I was left alone. I was just the "Casement skipper" who had a mental breakdown. I hung three towels at the foot of my bed. It kept the sergeant of the guard from being able to see me from the entryway. After several days of coming to my bunk and asking if I was there. I'd lift one trembling hand from underneath the blanket—he'd jog off. Every day I'd get up and walk with a stick. I imitated an elderly man, hobbling around the outskirts of the camp.

* * *

Our time had come. Our endless hours spent planning and preparing would now pay off. If everything went to plan. We'd arrive at the aerodrome in five hours. We smuggled enough supplies for a twenty-four-hour walk. We had plenty of bread, English cash, and even a couple of folding knives. We did not have wire cutters. We had heavy gloves to help us yank out the security fencing.

If we arrived at the aerodrome during daylight, we'd use the two calfskin aviators' caps and flying goggles we'd collected. We'd wear our cowhide petticoats, goggles, and walk right through like we belonged. If the aerodrome had over forty sheds, no one would notice. W said the greatest danger we faced would be when we approached the German coast in a British plane. If all went to plan we would be home safely on German soil, July 12, 1917.

The next morning a tennis tournament was held. The prisoners against the guards. The entire camp would be distracted. Several huge wicker seats were carried onto the tennis grounds. The seats were thirty yards from the channel. W and I slunk from the chairs into the overgrown grass and laid in the channel. Everything had to go as planned. The sergeant must believe I was in my bed. W had convinced the other sergeant to overlook his absence with a fistful of cash and cigarettes. Would it work? How long of a start would we have? If we could remain unnoticed during the morning check—we'd be assured of success.

The game continued for hours. The court was full of noise: ball smacks, applause, insults and energy. A few times I heard footsteps approach. But never watchmen, and never close enough to betray our position. At dusk, the band played an outdoor show to close the tournament. It was almost time. The last song was one I will forever remember. "Farewell Companions, to horse, to horse."

ESCAPING OUR ENSNAREMENT

We waited in the trench until the evening prisoner check. I hoped the day's events had drained the guards' energy. If we didn't raise the alarm, it would be safe to continue. Silence. No alarm raised. No dogs barking, and no English guards massing in force to organize a search party—yet.

I gave W the signal to move forward and we both got up in a crouch. *Voices*. Footsteps came closer. We fell to our stomachs. My face bounced in the mud of the ravine and the top of my head stung from the heel of W's shoe. *Guards*. Did they see us? We waited again.

"Did you ever see anything so senseless?" I recognized the voice.

Another voice replied, "The Huns learned a tennis lesson today." The echo of laughter and footsteps got closer. They were walking over the tennis court toward our trench. My heart was in my throat. I pressed my eyes closed. I felt around in the mud for a sharp rock. I was getting out of this camp one way or another tonight.

The voices faded into the distance. They walked right

past us. We waited again. The clay base of the trench had a thin film of water. I turned my face to the right. It was cold, dirty, and uncomfortable. Small dark shapes crawled out of the openings. Dark-colored bugs, ants, and other insects crept through my hair and down the back of my neck. The tennis court was silent. I bit my lip to hold back any moans or gasps.

The grass next to us stirred. Was something in there? There was no wind. Was something or someone coming toward us? Just then a dark creepy crawly bug crossed over my face. My body trembled. It went into my left ear. The little bastard tunneled further in, I pushed my head against the bottom of W's feet to force myself not to move. I couldn't stand it anymore. I shook my head and turned over to get the bug out of my ear. The grass shifted again. I came face to face with a buck bunny staring down at me.

We communicated with each other in Morse code by tapping on the water to make signs. The pinnacle clock struck eleven. We'd spent over three hours lying in this trench. I raised my head and peeped around. It was dark. Trees outside of the fence gave an ominous glow. Only a faint red light from the guard tower illuminated the night.

We rose from our trench and crept toward the fence. The guard on perimeter watch had vanished or was probably asleep. We dropped to our stomachs and crawled through the grass. It felt good to stretch. The blood flowed through my body again. We crawled inch by inch. Only small delays to breathe and adjust our thick calfskin petticoats under our tunics. All this crawling was hard work.

It was at least a half hour before we reached the wicker chairs on the tennis court. Our packs were underneath them as agreed. We took our time to organize and ready our tools as silently as possible. W nodded at me and we crawled to the area of fence we'd marked as the least troublesome. We slithered along with twice as much weight on our backs as earlier. I was face to face with the wire. It looked much more tangled and sharp than my previous careless assessment.

I slid on the heavy gloves and tried to pull at the wires. No luck. The wires were snared in a complicated web under the dirt and overgrown grass. I yanked and pulled and twisted. Still nothing would budge. My calfskin petticoat did its job of taking the brunt of spikes and tears. But we were not making progress. How long could we continue like this?

We kept at it. The pinnacle clock struck twelve—midnight. We were supposed to be out by now. Voices again. Guards coming toward us. They were relieving the others for the next watch. What the hell were we going to do? We couldn't move forward or crawl backward. All we could do was lie here and wait to be caught. I pulled on the wire again. Blood dripped from inside my glove. I held my breath. *Calm, stay calm, must stay calm.*

A guard walked along the fence line whistling. He came right toward us. I turned over onto my stomach and shoved my face in the ground. I closed my eyes and counted the seconds. Thirty, sixty, ninety. Sweat ran into my eyes and stung. Some of the salty liquid ran into the corner of my mouth.

He walked right past us. He said something I couldn't make out and stopped at the guard box. I had enough. Time to get out of here. I shoved myself through the spiked wire. I didn't feel the cuts and bruises. I pushed through—inch by inch. I struggled to get to the outside wire. I made progress. I puffed and gasped, my body was energized with a strength, a determination to continue. The maze of wires was coming to an end. W pushed my legs from behind to help force my shaking, shivering body through.

We were almost through it. I rolled to my back and took W's wrists and yanked him the rest of the way through. Once I saw he was safe and outside of the wire. I closed my eyes and panted in the tall grass. I was depleted. W grabbed my arm and nodded in the direction of Nottingham. He was right. We couldn't waste any time here. We needed to put as much distance as possible between us and the camp—before all hell broke loose.

SEARCHING FOR THE AERODROME

We ran through the woods. We stopped at two tall old trees. One of them was rotted and empty. We stuffed our torn petticoats inside. Our civilian clothes underneath weren't too destroyed. With our English language skills, we hoped to pass ourselves off as citizens.

We continued on through the woods and arrived at the street that led from Donington to the Trent river. I'd committed all the maps to memory. I was an expert in the local geography—even though I'd never been out here before. The undergrowth was thick. We had to clear a path with our hands. It was so dark I barely saw my hands in front of my face.

I tore at the brambles and stepped on a large creature that grunted with rage. A resting dairy cow. I hopped back before I was gored by its horns. A field opened up before us and we ran into it. We hopped over six wooden walls and continued over the bumpy ground until we made it into the primitive road.

We stopped at looked at each other. We were both spent and panting for air. I was about to ask W if he thought we should continue through the woods, or take the road. *Voices.* I glanced over my shoulder. They were less than a hundred yards away, over where the street sloped down. Were they camp guards coming back from leave?

I followed W over a thistle fence into an enormous cornfield. A dog started barking. I couldn't tell from which direction. I wasn't going to stop and find out. We rushed forward in the dark. The dog's barking got louder. The men's voice faded. I stopped and looked around for the damn dog. No sign of my furry friend. I whistled softly. *Nothing.* Something stirred in front of me. I held my breath. A tall outline appeared. I cocked my arm back to strike. It was W.

We sat in the grass and caught our breath. The dog's barking stopped. The voices were gone. Everything was calm. I was so thirsty. All we had with us to drink were two little medication bottles filled with whiskey. This was not the time for that. We pushed on and jogged ahead into the night.

We came upon a stream and trudged forward. W cried out. He was up to his hips in a peat bog. I was right behind him and sinking fast. I couldn't see my legs past my thighs. We moved backward. I cycled my legs like I rode a bike. I reached for anything to pull myself out. I crawled out of the bog and helped pull W out. Just a few feet farther in and we would not have escaped.

We laid in the lowland reeds. Our only box of matches had gotten wet. We couldn't see far in front of us. We chose to follow the stream as a guide. After a half hour we came to a railroad line. The line forked a hundred yards in front of us. Where did these rails lead? I didn't remember any railroad intersection on my map. My best guess was that the left fork would lead us to the Trent river. We climbed the high fences that flanked the railroad and followed the line to the left. Was this the right choice?

Daybreak dawned in the East. We should have been at the aerodrome by now. Something sparkled through the trees on the right—water. Finally, the Trent river. We jumped in and crossed it in less than a minute. Hope surged through me. On this side of the Trent it looked uninhabited. It was almost dawn when we arrived at the crossroads. A battered sign post showed us we were twelve miles out of our way. *Damn.* We needed to make up for lost time and ground. My body was tired. My mind was ready to march on. But my legs could barely move.

We continued on at a slower pace. After a little drop of whiskey and a corner of chocolate, we were resuscitated. I would have killed for water. We entered into a neighborhood. We passed workers that looked at us in surprise and disgust. I mumbled a "hello" and trudged on. The plan was to remain as invisible as we could.

An upper class Englishman stopped to ask us if we'd seen a pony and a truck pass by. I said no. I felt the man's eyes on the back of us as we passed. It gave me an awkward, eerie feeling. We hoped to give off the impression we were on our way to work. It wasn't long before we past the last house in town and were back out in the open.

We stayed on the railroad line and followed it to the south toward Nottingham. We must be close now. I felt invigorated and ready to climb into a plane to freedom. We continued on for another two hours. No planes in the sky. Nothing to suggest that a flying ground was anywhere close. Where was it? I conjured up a mental image of that map still fresh in my mind from months of study. We were in the right place, we had to be close. The aerodrome had to be within two miles of our present location. But where?

"Listen," W said. He pointed to the sky.

A biplane approached from the north. A German biplane. In seconds he was over us. He must have been above twelve-hundred feet as he passed us. We followed his course like statues, waiting to see where he'd land. He flew on his current heading until he was a speck in the sky. Should we rest? Continue on our current course? Was the aerodrome even where we thought it was? Had Germany invaded?

We continued on. The sun was savage and my face felt like it was on fire. My throat was tight. I couldn't make any saliva to swallow. I dreamed of a cool glass of water. Something loomed up ahead. A manufacturing plant hidden by tall shrubs. Where were we? We crept toward the plant for a better look. A foul, dingy stream stood in our way. Voices and movement not far away. I had no idea where we were now. But it was time to get away from here.

We sat down in the shadows of some thick, high brambles. W sucked the dampness from the stalks of grass. I was so tired. We settled on taking a short rest here.

W shook me awake after what seemed like minutes. A yapping dog was getting louder. Were we followed? The camp must know of our disappearance by now. Was this the search party? I poked my head over the shrubs and scanned the area. A kid was playing with a dog as they walked down the street. I slunk around the shrub and got in front of the kid and his dog.

I dropped a sixpence in the street and pretended to be looking for something when the pair approached me. The kid eagerly helped me look for my coin and when he found it, I gave it to him for his trouble. I asked him if he'd known about the pilot that'd crashed in the area not long ago. The kid was no help. He didn't know anything, but I gleaned that a flying ground must be somewhere close by. The kid pointed in a direction it might be but had no detailed knowledge of where.

He pointed me in the direction of Nottingham and said there were two daily trains to London. I gave him a cigarette and pretended I was leaving. After he'd gone, I circled back to W and filled him in on the details. We'd need to walk through the night to avoid being seen. We were getting into little villages and towns and stuck out.

Our lack of water was unbearable. We pondered on entering one of the houses we passed and asking inside for water. But it was too dangerous. We found a pool of grimy water that looked like it was for dairy cattle. We hurled ourselves onto it and drank. We shared our lone tin of frankfurter. We'd not seen any vegetables in the fields—only grass, soiled canals, and security fencing. Our clothes were filthy and getting torn to shreds. W had brought along sewing materials to repair our clothes.

* * *

FOR THREE DAYS we wandered through the area looking for the aerodrome. It was not where we'd thought. It wasn't anywhere. Our secondary choice of aerodromes was farther away. We'd need to take the train to get closer to it. We could hide in a merchandise car as stowaways. Our escape would mean that the railroad yards and trains would be more heavily watched.

We spent one more night searching for the missing aerodrome. We hid behind little shrubs and ate pieces of chicken feed left in the fields. Still nothing. Our food reserves were almost gone. Two cuts of stale dry bread and no water. We decided it was time to get to Nottingham. We'd get some food there and then make our way to London and sneak onto the huge aerodrome at Hendon.

Why were the English not pursuing us? They must have known about our escape by now. Were they waiting to get us back without making a fuss? Were we just lucky? We continued on. The streets became less abandoned and little estates dotted the sides of the road. We were walking into an enormous town—Nottingham.

Workman passed us on the road and a cyclist asked us for directions. I gave him directions like I'd lived here my whole life, although I have no idea where I sent him.

We turned a corner and came face to face with a police officer. I shoved my hands deep into my pockets. I looked down and without a word passed him by. Out of the corner of my eye the police officer looked us both up and down but didn't say a word. A loud plane buzzed overhead and diverted his attention. An enormous biplane followed the Trent river at around 300 feet. Was he looking for us? Were the English authorities searching?

On the left side of the street we came upon a little ranch house. A kid—the same kid with the dog—smiled and waved at us from the roadside. I asked him if this was his house, and if so would he sell us food. He ducked into the house and returned a few moments later, telling us to come inside. W shook his head and wanted no part of it. I had a good feeling and suggested he stay outside as a lookout.

I walked inside and a round woman in her thirties greeted me, "Decent evening, sir," and motioned for me to have a seat in the kitchen. We made chit chat which turned to the war and the fate of the *doomed Germans*. She handed me a cup of the best tea I'd ever drank. She handed me a bundle of cream-cheddar bread wrapped in lettuce leaves and a large jug of tea. I pushed a few coins over the table to her and rushed off with my treasure like a dog with a bone.

We'd never eaten this good since our captivity in England. We must have looked like wild animals gorging ourselves under the tree—savoring our first meal in days. I called the kid over, gave him the empty tea jug and asked about the low flying biplane we saw earlier. The kid filled us in about the enormous aerodrome north of Nottingham on the opposite side of the Trent river. Why didn't he tell us before? He also went on to say how the little aerodrome by the railroad had been shut for over a month. I bit my lip before I cursed in his face. Our last few days had been pointless. *What a waste*. How would I have known?

We had the info we needed to find the next aerodrome. Time to trudge our way there, it wouldn't be much farther now. I had a full stomach, a renewed sense of hope, I bursted with energy to get to the aerodrome and make my way home.

LIGHTS OF NOTTINGHAM

We were back at the Trent river. In this spot it was twice as wide as before. Time to swim again, but I couldn't raise my arms over my chest. I needed to rest. We could make our way into Nottingham in the morning. A neighboring field laid a few hundred yards off to the right. We settled in to rest.

Not even two hours later, the sky darkened, and the wind whistled. The temperature dropped at least ten degrees. *Rain*. A stream of water ran through the field. Everything became wet and moist. We hopped up and followed the lights to Nottingham.

We arrived in town as the morning unfolded. The roads were jammed with workman walking to their processing plants. We joined in with a horde of fifty laborers. We passed various police along the way that didn't even give us a second glance. We passed through the main thoroughfare in town. Ugly little red houses and several plant smoke-stacks. The roads weren't kept well, and we avoided the mud and potholes like mines.

A small elderly man with bowed shoulders jabbed at sacks of garbage with his stick. He'd find something of interest and brush it off and put it into his pack. W grabbed my arm and pointed at the notice sheets on the side of a wall.

CONSIDERATION!

DANGEROUS GERMAN OFFICERS ESCAPED FROM DONINGTON HALL ON SATURDAY EVENING.

KARL SPINDLER — GERMAN NAVY OFFICER, 30, HAIR DULL, EYES BLUE, STRONG CONSTRUCTED, 5 FT. 11 IN., CLEAN-SHAVEN, TALKS ENGLISH, DRESS PRESUMABLY REGULAR CITIZEN.

ERNST WINKELMANN — GERMAN PILOT, 23, HAIR DULL EARTHY COLORED, EYES EARTHY COLORED, THINLY CONSTRUCTED, 5 FT. 10 IN., CLEAN-SHAVEN, TALKS ENGLISH, DRESS MOST LIKELY REGULAR CITIZEN, JAWBONES BROKEN BY SLUG.

It was only a matter of time. Saturday evening? They must have known we'd escaped well before then. Could they really be that incompetent? We were getting closer now. The cable car lines led us the rest of the way into town. It was around 7 a.m. and the boulevards were coming to life. We drifted away from our massive group and I bought a couple cigarettes from a store. I asked for directions to the aerodrome. Just on the other side of the river across a bridge. Only steps away, I was tempted to run.

We hurried toward the bridge and came face to face with

a closed gate. Two police officers stood off to the left side. Were they looking for us? Or just checking through the workers? Where was that mob of people now? Better to wait for that horde of workman and blend in with them across the bridge. We found an inviting field down a side street with a view of the bridge and plunked down to wait on a bench.

After ten minutes, two police officers came up the road with three manacled prisoners. The cling and clang echoed in the field as they marched right by us. I pulled out a scratch pad and pretended to write figures and include W in conversation. They passed by without acknowledging us. *Lucky*. That could have easily been us chained up and marched back to Donington Camp.

I eased my shoulders and I released my breath. Then I heard, "Left wheel. Walk." They came right at us. I stood up to answer his questions. They all rushed us. Even the chained men. It happened so fast I had no time to process it. All five men held us down. They transferred the shackles onto W and me. I recognized the old man with the stick. Was it he that betrayed us? Were we lured into a trap? How long had they been following us?

I asked the officer to let me sit up. I was chained to W and surrounded by five men. Where did they think we would go? The officer in charge nodded his head. We pushed ourselves up against a tree. The questioning began.

"I don't recognize you." The older officer with a white handlebar mustache asked. "What are you doing around here?"

I sat up straighter and nodded to W. "My name's Grieve, and this is Kendall. We're mechanics. Going to the aerodrome to work."

"Where you live?" The officer crinkled his lips.

I hesitated. What was the name of that village we passed? *Damn.* I opened my mouth to say something and he put his massive hand on my shoulder.

He said, "No, sir. You're Captain Spindler, and he's Winkelmann from Donington Hall, right?"

I stared at him. I was caught. W cursed in German to seal our fate. I nodded and said, "yes sir, well done. Well done, indeed."

The old officer was taken back and seemed impressed. His tune changed and he treated us with respect. He undid our shackles and asked us to follow him. At least we wouldn't be chained like common criminals and led through town on display. We were caught. Any further attempt to escape from here would be futile.

We didn't have far to walk. The police station was less than a hundred yards from our bench in the field. At police headquarters we were searched, and all our possessions confiscated. The new investigator questioning us was astonished we had a map of the area.

"You think you'd just walk right in and fly a plane to Germany?" The investigator flung the map on the stained wooden table in front of us.

I shrugged.

He continued, "we cautioned the aerodromes that you might try something. You would have been shot on sight."

I yawned.

After several more minutes of lecture and questions he seemed satisfied. He ordered the uniformed English soldiers standing by to "take us out." We were led out in chains to a large lorry truck. We stopped at different police stations along the way to pick up more prisoners. After the lorry was loaded up with twenty four prisoners, she lurched to a police base camp.

I was separated from W and taken to a proper cell with solid iron bars. Guards and soldiers stood and stared. They gave contemptuous looks and referred to me a "German dog." Minutes later a constable showed up and was ushered inside. He treated me with the respect I was due. He complimented me on my cunning break and asked if I needed anything.

I asked for a warm breakfast and a couple of cigarettes. He waved to one of the guards and in minutes I had a cigarette dangling from my lip, black tea, and a full breakfast in front of me. He would represent me in the court proceeding and was interested to know who helped us get away and along the way to Nottingham.

I shook my head and lied. "No one helped us. We got by on our wits and luck." I took a deep drag of my cigarette. "Our luck ran out."

The old man nodded and smiled.

After I finished my breakfast, I was brought into the English court. Would they execute me for escape? We followed a parade of men blamed for robbery and other crimes. We were the highlight of the day. Onlookers crowded in to see. W sat next to me, his head was down, and he didn't say a word. A man announced to the crowd that the two Hun officers had been recaptured.

Another more formal interrogation began. The court would not accept that we'd gotten away on Thursday and not on Saturday. They continued asking the same questions for a week straight trying to understand. They couldn't comprehend how we'd done it with the number of guards and an electric wire fence. Luckily for us, the electric fence had been down for weeks. I answered their questions honestly, except for the details of our getaway. That was my secret, I'd guard it until long after this ordeal was over.

We had twelve men escort us. Some were the Donington prison watchmen. They filled us in on the missing details of how we were found out. It wasn't until the next day that another prisoner—Horn—was caught trying to escape through the wire fence. He didn't make it through and was stuck on a spike screaming for help. After he was brought back and interrogated, he informed them of our plans to get to the aerodrome and fly home. He ruined our escape. *Stupid.* Why did I tell him our plans?

After he returned to the prison, Donington hall snapped into action. They terrified the nation and mobilized men to watch the railroad stations and aerodromes. They assembled hundreds of men to search for us. Police officers on bikes, horses, aviators, and investigators—all on the hunt for us.

Nottingham was put on an even higher alert. Special government investigators were sent to assist the police. It was them who found us. We again made the papers as infamous celebrities. The headline read:

Two escaped German officers from Donington recovered!

We were brought back to Donington hall after our court appearances. We arrived to whistling, applause, and congratulations. Even the prison guards were not as upset as I'd imagined them to be. While they wasted no time in describing in detail how our escape had caused them much distress—the fine name of Donington was tarnished—no one had ever gotten as far away as we did. We were put into separate confinement cells for three weeks. We were to wait in isolation on the decision of the military court.

The constable in the courthouse had told me to expect

at least six months of isolation. Maybe more because we'd studied the location of the aerodromes. They may want to make an example out of me for the other German officers. There was a chance I could be hanged. I was kept in an isolated cell for fourteen days waiting on word of my fate.

TWO YEARS OF SLAVERY

I was transferred to another camp—Holyport—because It was too dangerous to keep me in Donington. The new commandant was an old Indian Army man. He requested to see me. What an awful old man. It was clear from his manner he was repulsed by me and he snarled whenever he saw me. He ordered that I be kept in isolation.

In November I was summoned to the English prize court. I had an escort of eight men with pikes surround me. I was taken to a military detainment center at Cromwell Gardens where I waited for two weeks. I was informed I was going on trial. What was I on trial for now?

The filthy, frosty cell at Cromwell Gardens wore on my spirit. The guards there treated me with no respect. From my cell on the fourth floor, the window had just enough of an opening to get a sliver of sight outside. Was I in the South Kensington region? The area outside was ravaged. Busted buildings, crumbling churches, the shelling had been intense. Was I here as a shield against further assaults?

The next day a lorry was sent to bring me to the prize court. Sir Samuel Evans and Attorney-General, Sir Frederick

Smith, led the case against me. I was to be charged with sedition and murder. They accused me of being a spy and demanded I should share the same fate as Sir Roger Casement. I was on display for a room full of judges, translators, and pressmen. I was not allowed to defend myself or speak. This was a war crime.

In three hours I was back on that same lorry to jail. The food was pitiful. Two pieces of bread twice a day with watery tea, oily soup with either rotten herring or slim potatoes. The mug it was served in was slimy and had no handle. My bed was a torn straw-sleeping pad spotted with old blood-stains.

So, back on trial for the *Aud*. I was again referred to as the "Casement skipper" and the subject of jeering, surly guards. One Irish watchmen turned out to be an ally. He had no love for the English and applauded my effort to help "the cause." From him I learned of the German captives taken from the annihilated submarines. I was able to buy better food and cigarettes from him—he even gave me cash from one of my mates.

The next day my cell door opened, and uniformed soldiers came to take me. They refused to say where or why. I recognized the route from the back of the lorry. The imposing gate of Donington hall loomed ahead. The entire prison awaited my return in the courtyard.

The camp commandant took all my cash and possessions. My case was excused. If I tried to escape again. I'd be shot. I was left with nothing but the filthy clothes I wore during my escape.

In the months that followed I developed a skin condition from the grimy sleeping cushion and fell ill.

After two more years of misery, pain, and captivity—I was traded in a prisoner exchange and sent to Holland.

FINAL NOTE

Captain Karl Spindler barely survived his final years of captivity in England. He arrived in the Netherlands in a weakened state of ill-health and took months to recover. He was awarded several medals for his bravery and was promoted to a Section Chief in the Naval Command.

He went on tour telling the story of the *Aud-Norge* and became a celebrity. He earned a cult like following in the US. In 1931 to commemorate the 15th anniversary of the Irish Easter Rising. The Irish committee president in New York invited Spindler for a lecture tour in New York, Philadelphia, Chicago, Pittsburgh, Detroit, Boston and other cities..

The main event took place on Easter Sunday in the city of San Francisco. Immediately on entering the city there was a parade. Market Street was draped with banners welcoming Captain Spindler to the city. They gave him a medal struck in pure gold with his portrait and an inscription that read "who in 1916 risked his life for Irish liberty."

Although he returned to Germany to see his family, Spindler remained in the United States for the rest of his life. During World War II he was detained in an internment camp as an enemy alien. He never achieved permanent residency or naturalization in the US. He was released in poor health at the end of the war.

Karl Spindler died on November 29, 1951 in Bismarck, North Dakota.

ALSO BY WAR HISTORY JOURNALS

Broken Wings: WWI Fighter Ace's Story of Escape and Survival

"A masterfully told story of triumph and redemption in a powerfully drawn survival epic." – Reviewer

Hero WWI Fighter Pilot Shot Down and Captured.

With an engaging and authentic retelling of his experiences as an escaped prisoner of war, this gripping account details the life and struggles of a captured pilot in 1917 war-torn Europe.

Lieutenant John Ryan couldn't wait to see action in WWI. He joined up with the British colors out of Canada. As one of several American pilots in the Royal Flying Corps before the US joined the war, he earned his wings and became an Ace through fierce air battles over the skies of Germany.

Journey into Eden: WWI Adventures in the Mesopotamian Motor Machine Gun Corps

"Having served in Iraq, the comparisons to Wooten's World War I experiences with my own were remarkable." – Reviewer

Uncover a fascinating glimpse into WWI on the Mesopotamian front.

Few people truly know about Iraq's role in World War One. The stage of a desperate struggle against the Ottomans, the story of brave men who lived and served in this harsh landscape is often overshadowed by the battles in Europe and North Africa.

But now, this memoir explores the life and duty of Frank Wooten, an American, serving as a British officer in the Mesopotamian

Motor Machine Gun Corps. Told with gripping detail and offering profound insights into the lesser-known Middle Eastern theater, this book provides a unique perspective of the war to end all wars.

Recounting Frank's daily life on the front, his duties throughout the war, and the incredible people he met along the way, *Journey into Eden* is a fascinating book, perfect for anyone interested in the lesser-known stories of World War One, the history of the Iraq War, and the nature of life on the front.

World at War: Unforgettable Tales from the First and Second World Wars

"True Stories of Endurance, Horror and Beautiful Human Beings." – Reviewer

Haunting Truths We Must Never Forget.

Follow in the footsteps of the British, German and American servicemen as they detail the life and struggles of war in mysterious and foreign countries. Uncover their mesmerizing, realistic stories of combat, courage, and distress in readable and balanced stories told from the front lines.

This book brings you firsthand accounts of combat and brotherhood, of captivity and redemption, and the aftermath of wars that left no community unscathed in the world. These stories have everything from spies and snipers to submarines and air raids. A great book for anyone who wants to learn what it was like during the world war conflicts between 1914-1945.

CPSIA information can be obtained
at www.ICGtesting.com
Printed in the USA
BVHW030950301220
596746BV00001B/161

9 781393 306023